THE ANDORRA AND SECRET ENCLAVES & THE GIBRALTAR REPORT

UNDISCOVERED FISCAL PARADISES OF THE PYRENEES

THIRD EDITION

REVISED & EXPANDED

FOR 1994

Dr. W.G. Hill

SCOPE INTERNATIONAL LIMITED

Published by
Scope International Ltd.,
62 Murray Road,
Waterlooville,
Hants PO8 9JL
Great Britain

3rd Edition 1994
By Dr W.G. Hill

For questions and further information contact the publisher.

British Library Cataloguing in-Publication Data.
Hill, William G.
The Andorra and Gibraltar report.
1. Tax havens
I. Title
336.206

ISBN 0-906619-31-9

Phototypeset by Barbara James Typesetting, Rowlands Castle, Hampshire
Printed by Hartnolls, Bodmin, Cornwall

CONTENTS

THE ANDORRA REPORT

9
10
11
12
F
G
H
I
J
EASTERN BEACH
EASTERN BEACH RD
VIEWPOINT
CATALAN BAY
CATALAN VILLAGE
CATALAN BAY RD
WATER CATCHMEN
NORTH FRONT CEMETERY
VIEWPOINT
UPPER GALLERIES
SIGNAL STATION RD
BORDER
AIRPORT TERMINAL
DEVIL'S TOWER RD
CROSS OF SACRIFICE
VIEWPOINT
VIEWPOINT
QUEEN'S RD
OLD QU
VICTORIA STADIUM
WINSTON CHURCHILL AVE
MOORISH CASTLE
BAYSIDE RD
WILLIS'S RD
DEVIL'S GAP STPS
HOSPITAL
FLAT BASTION RD
GARDIN
PRINCE EDWARD'S RD
PRINCE EDWARD'S RD
WESTERN BEACH
GLACIS RD
SMITH DORRIEN AVE
CASEMATES
ENGINEER LANE
GOVERNOR'S ST
MAIN STREET
MAIN STREET
GOVERNOR'S RESIDENCE
FISH MARKET RD
IRISH TOWN
BOMB HSE LANE
POLICE
LINE WALL RD
LINE WALL RD
QUEENSWAY
QUEENSWAY
COACH PARK
GIBRALTAR MUSEUM
MARINAS
NORTH MOLE

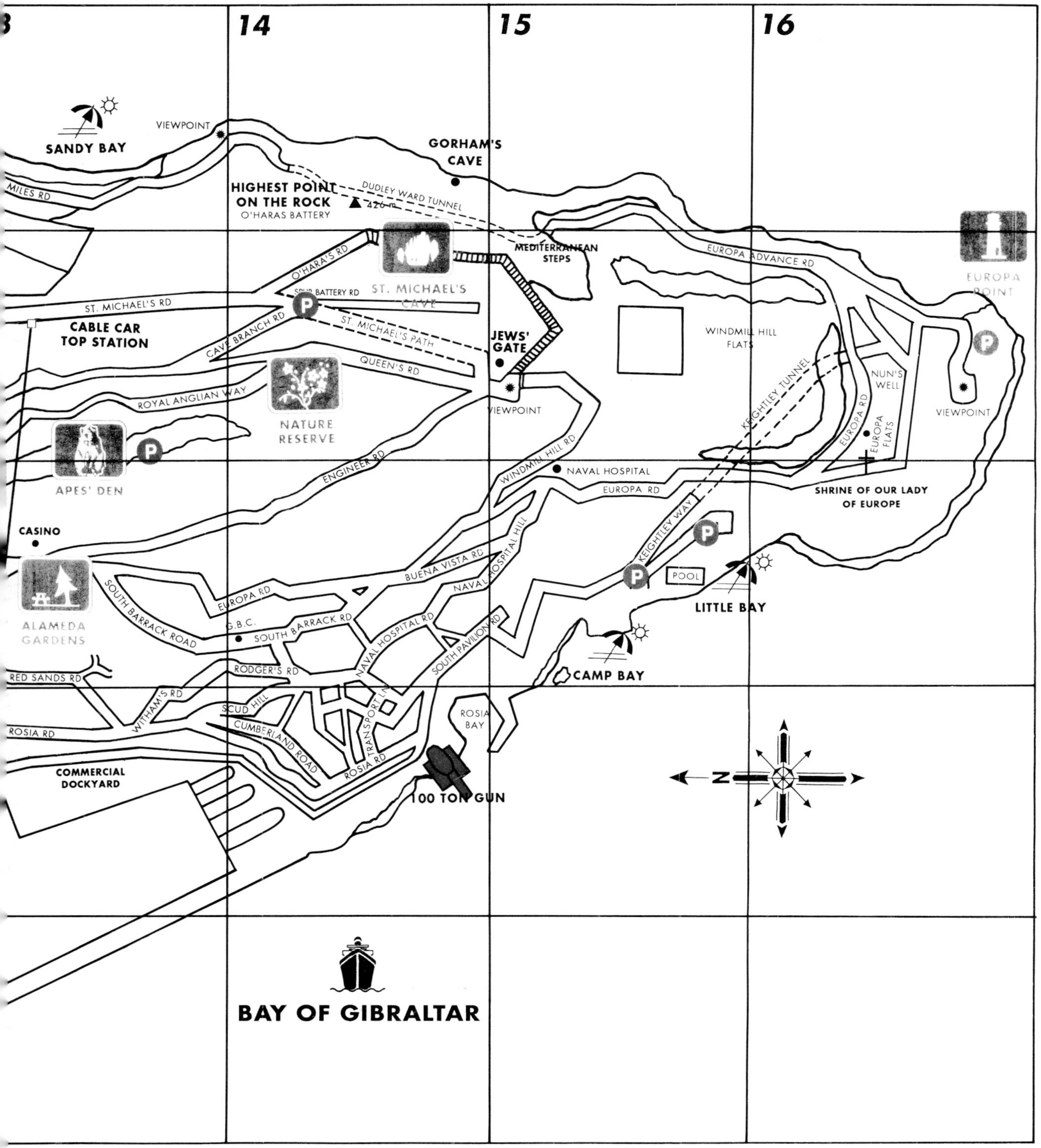

14
15
16
SANDY BAY
VIEWPOINT
GORHAM'S CAVE
MILES RD
HIGHEST POINT ON THE ROCK
O'HARAS BATTERY
426 m
DUDLEY WARD TUNNEL
MEDITERRANEAN STEPS
EUROPA ADVANCE RD
EUROPA POINT
O'HARA'S RD
SPUR BATTERY RD
ST. MICHAEL'S CAVE
ST. MICHAEL'S RD
CABLE CAR TOP STATION
CAVE BRANCH RD
ST. MICHAEL'S PATH
JEWS' GATE
WINDMILL HILL FLATS
QUEEN'S RD
ROYAL ANGLIAN WAY
NATURE RESERVE
VIEWPOINT
KEIGHTLEY TUNNEL
NUN'S WELL
EUROPA RD
EUROPA FLATS
VIEWPOINT
APES' DEN
ENGINEER RD
WINDMILL HILL RD
NAVAL HOSPITAL
EUROPA RD
SHRINE OF OUR LADY OF EUROPE
CASINO
KEIGHTLEY WAY
BUENA VISTA RD
NAVAL HOSPITAL HILL
POOL
LITTLE BAY
ALAMEDA GARDENS
SOUTH BARRACK ROAD
EUROPA RD
G.B.C.
SOUTH BARRACK RD
NAVAL HOSPITAL RD
SOUTH PAVILION RD
CAMP BAY
RED SANDS RD
RODGER'S RD
WITHAM'S RD
SCUD HILL
TRANSPORT LN
ROSIA BAY
ROSIA RD
CUMBERLAND ROAD
ROSIA RD
COMMERCIAL DOCKYARD
100 TON GUN
N
BAY OF GIBRALTAR

ANDORRA & GIBRALTAR: INTRODUCTION

When Johnny Lunchbucket talks of retiring, he thinks of Spain, Portugal or Italy. Forsythe Financier thinks of Bermuda or Monaco. Who considers Andorra or Gibraltar? Both are relatively-undiscovered tax havens offering southern European climate and atmosphere. Gibraltar is densely populated. Andorra is rural and picturesque.

You'll find the autonomous secluded Pyrenees mountain Principality of Andorra, a no-nuke, no-tax haven, on the French-Spanish border. Facing Africa on the southern coast of Spain is the British Crown Colony of Gibraltar, an up-and-coming offshore financial center. Both are rated by us as possible places to live for a PT (prior taxpayer).

Andorra is a personal tax haven. Property is still affordable. Living costs are low. Natural beauty, powder snow in winter, miles of ski and hiking trails, plus low prices on a huge selection of foodstuffs and consumer durables are attractive features.

Gibraltar is the place for your offshore company to be domiciled. Gibraltar is easy to reach by plane, bus, car or boat.

Andorra is a little off the beaten path. But this is not a bad thing if/when life in big cities gets rough. It's a place to actually settle in, to escape economic depression, rampant AIDS, random violence and police intimidation. No nuclear plants are in the vicinity. The absence of leftist political parties and any hint of a "socialist mentality" earns Andorra another couple of points.

On the sunny south side of Spain is Gibraltar. Only three square miles (six square kilometers), this historic mountain rock is the only British Crown Colony left in Europe. It has been dubbed the "Thirteenth country of the EC".

Taxwise, Gibraltar is not a true tax haven like Andorra. Even though "The Rock" is considered a tax haven by many, this is mainly for non-resident and other tax-exempt Gibraltar companies. We will discuss this important distinction in more detail later. Individuals habitually resident or domiciled on Gibraltar will find that it DOES have an income tax. Since the socialists took over in 1985, the progressive income tax has been raised to its current maximum of 50 per cent. The max tax bracket is reached when your net annual income exceeds £20,000 after plentiful deductions. This 50 per cent tax exists in theory. No one but poor unfortunate wage-slaves pay this max tax. Most Gibraltarians pay no more than the minimum basic rate of 20 per cent. If you, as a PT, decide to make Gibraltar your home base, personal income taxes are easily avoided so long as you do not have any LOCAL SOURCE INCOME. In PT-speak "local source income", just in case you forgot, means operating a visible local business or visible professional office. If you run a consulting operation for foreigners or manage foreign investments for foreigners from your Gibraltar apartment, there is no great risk of being asked to pay any taxes at all.

Gibraltar tax officials are like those of Italy or Costa Rica. If there is no visible local business activity, they do not bother the relatively-few rich foreigners who live there. This contrasts with France, Scandinavia or the United States where the mere local ownership of a deluxe apartment or a conspicuous car will eventually result in a "friendly visit" from tax collectors. They may then assess an income tax based upon lifestyle. In Paris, if you can't prove you have another fiscal residence where you A) Pay taxes, or B) Spend more time than you do in France, you can expect your house or car to be seized and sold for back taxes. These taxes are assessed quite arbitrarily. Spain, unfortunately, is gearing up to follow the grabby example of France, the USA and other ruthless tax-driven regimes. As the computer-age comes to the Spanish Income Tax Office, land or car or hacienda ownership (as in France) will automatically generate tax bills based upon certain assumptions arising from the value of the home or car involved. For instance, France estimates the "rental value" of your home or apartment, and then arbitrarily assesses taxes on an assumed income of five times that amount. A car may be assumed to be the equivalent of six-months' income. Once tax bills are sent out, the burden falls upon the taxpayer to prove he is a non-resident or that money he spends to support his lifestyle is somehow exempt from income tax under local law. Failing to do this, the taxpayer's local property is at risk. It can be leined, seized and eventually sold for taxes. In the USA, not only property is at risk. Your freedom is also in danger. Elderly Aldo Gucci, of Milan, found himself with a one year jail term in California for what USA authorities dubbed tax fraud. Aldo's defense was: "I have been doing the same thing in Italy for 70 years".

HOW TO STAY OFF COMPUTERS. FOREVER!

Because we never know what changes may be made in the rules of the game, the newsletter author Harry D Schultz, advises that a true PT should never own a car, home or apartment at all.

Nor should one ever vote. In the Schultz view, staying off government computers – any government computer – should be one of the main objects in the game of life. The Hill view is that so long as a car or a home is modest and is viewed as disposable, there is no great harm in owning one.

In places like Gibraltar, Italy and even Spain or Portugal as of now, the government is not going to risk scaring off its tourist business by anything so drastic as the seizure of property from those who appear to be mere seasonal visitors (Perennial Tourists). For an additional degree of safety, property or cars can be kept in a company name, partnership or other legal entity with a different name from your own. But your author agrees that like bank accounts, cars and homes should always be registered in the name of individuals or entities with addresses outside the country where one lives, keeps or actually drives the vehicle.

A MILLION EXPATS ARE YOUR NEIGHBORS

Living in Andorra or in Gibraltar means enjoying the dry California-like climate of sunny southern Europe but without the government hassles of USA, Spain or Portugal. An estimated 1 million English-speaking expatriates have made the Iberian peninsula their home. Most live on Spain's Costa Del Sol. Portugal is the number two choice for retirees or vacation home owners.

Southern Europe sports low (Spain) or very low (Portugal) prices on almost everything except high-tech or imported manufactured goods. The two countries offer some of Europe's most historic scenery and old castles. Give the Spaniards and the Portuguese credit for having "discovered", explored, mapped and colonised most of the world.

Living in sunny Iberia these days, however, is not without its troubles. The Latinos like putting off tasks. Getting almost any tiny little job done means getting a permit and dealing with a lot of "pay-me-off-before-I'll-help-you" style bureaucrats.

Anyone who's ever tried to do any business in Spain or Portugal will certify that "The Great Iberian Paper-Chase" is an ageing experience. Efficient banking in Spain or Portugal is impossible. If you ever find your way through the maze of currency regulations, restrictions and government reporting forms, you're faced with waiting the better part of an hour for nothing more than a simple cash withdrawal.

Incompetent, corrupt government officials are a problem for the Iberian economies as well as the cause of the backward workings of their financial sector. This, coupled with an annual inflation rate of some 10 to 15 per cent, makes the Iberian peninsula look like just about the worst place in Europe for banking your money. Especially if you live there.

No need to worry, though. In the following pages, we are about to discover the joys of Iberian living without the downside. You are about to learn the secrets of undiscovered Andorra and Gibraltar . . .

GIBRALTAR

THE GIBRALTAR REPORT

Gibraltar, ''The Rock of Gibraltar'', is a part of the European Community yet is exempt from VAT taxes. Recently it has become a fairly important center for offshore banking and mutual fund management. It is a well known tax-haven for ''offshore'' corporations and is considered by some as a tax-haven for individuals to live in as well.

Primarily a British military base, Gibraltar is well known to the million annual vacationers visiting southern Spain. They all flock to the supermarkets on Gibraltar's Main Street at least once per vacation. Why? To stock up on British bangers (breakfast sausages), Aunt Jemima Pancake Mix, Log Cabin Syrup, HJ Heinz tinned soups, Branston Pickles and many other favorites not to be found in Spain. On the three-mile length of Main Street (or shopping street) there are several UK banks. The only Gibraltar known to tourists and day-trippers is just this one long busy street of pubs, fish 'n' chips, and tax-free shops. Prices on groceries and consumer goods (jewelry, watches, cameras, hi-fi, etc.) are 30 per cent to 40 per cent below London rates.

There are not many rental apartments on the market these days. But the diligent looker will, with a bit of sniffing, be able to find rentals in all price ranges. Likewise as to condominiums for sale. As in Monaco, the limited space available has meant that there are very few single family homes (or ''villas'' as they are known locally). These properties come on the market more rarely than apartments. But the situation is comparable to Monaco or Campione. If one moves to a hotel and spends a few weeks looking around, suitable accommodations can always be found – at a price that is around double the cost of similar accommodation right across the border in Spain.

So why not live in Spain? In Spain the selection is infinitely greater. Nearby Sotogrande, for instance, is a golf club development primarily for Brits and other foreigners. A comfortable two bedroom home with yard, swimming pool (right on the fairway) might be picked up for around -£80,000 or rented for some £700 monthly. Golf membership in the country club included!

For £80,000, in Gibraltar, one could only get a small condominium, no pool, in a new (but tacky) apartment building far too near the busy airport.

This is one of the reasons that for every foreigner who buys a home or apartment in Gibraltar, perhaps 10,000 buy or rent in southern Spain. The buyers in Spain are primarily people who want a vacation home or place to retire in the relatively warm, sunny California desert-like climate. If they are PTs they have consciously thought about taxes. They avoid the Spanish income tax levy on their world-wide income. How? They never become registered permanent residents of Spain. Property is registered in a Gibraltar or Liechtenstein company. Car registration and legal domicile is maintained elsewhere. Where? In a place like Sark perhaps. See our Channel Island Report, summarised at the back of this book.

Is Gibraltar a good place for your domicile? Only under certain limited circumstances. Here's what's wrong with Gibraltar.

First, those who live in Gibraltar and want to go to Spain regularly must cross an international frontier. This is a disputed frontier. Since its reopening in 1984/85 it has been chronically afflicted with long queues and tailbacks due to "go-slows" and obsessive passport and customs checking by Spanish border personnel. Leaving Gibraltar, there is usually a car search. As a result, crossing the border into Spain often takes an hour or more. This frustrating situation will probably continue as long as the status of Gibraltar is subject to dispute between Spain and the UK. In the past, the sealed border made a ferry boat ride of several hours (or a shorter plane trip) via Morocco necessary if a Gibraltar person wanted to visit a Spanish friend or play golf just half a mile away.

Should you live in nearby Spain?

The Spanish towns just across the frontier have an acute unemployment problem. There are many drug addicts. This results in high rates of violent crime, burglary and petty theft. Thirdly, English-speaking families will no doubt wish to avail themselves of an education to British standards for their children; Spanish residents' children may not attend Gibraltar schools.

Thus the higher priced living facilities of Gibraltar when compared to Spain have a few advantages. Also, Gibraltar property can probably be sold faster because there is considerable demand and very little supply of new or desirable housing. Office space is equally in short supply. But for most people, a "vacation home" in Spain at Sotogrande golf course or near the luxury Puerto Banus is a more pleasant arrangement than actually living in Gibraltar. Legal residence or domicile plus car registration should be in a third country.

FINANCIAL ADVANTAGES OF GIBRALTAR

Living in Gibraltar gives you a few financial advantages. There are no capital gains taxes nor property taxes and no death duties. There are no exchange controls nor double taxation agreements with any other country. A code of secrecy regarding banking transactions is enforced. Of course, one does not have to live in Gibraltar to have a Gibraltar holding company or bank account.

If one prefers living in the ambience of a rundown ethnic London suburb with water views, Gibraltar has all the newspapers, magazines, restaurants, pubs, and ambience of working class Britain. It also has British Broadcasting Corporation radio and TV programmes coming in loud and clear. Gibraltar is tied into the efficient British Telecom system. Thus for those who want relatively cheap communication and direct dial to London facilities, Gibraltar is better than Spain. Also, there is an incredibly cheap daily jet-flight from Gibraltar to London. The flight takes under three hours. Round trips cost around £100 to £150 depending upon whether you go charter or scheduled. Local travel agents are always coming up with cheap last minute bargain deals on flights, cruises, vacation packages, just as they do in the famous "bucket shops" of London. So, Gibraltar is a good place to be "from" for a PT with lots of leisure time and a desire for budget-travel. Do you fancy a spur-of-the-moment all expenses two-week trip to Gambia, Malta or some other exotic place for half the price of the hotel rooms alone? Gibraltar is almost as good as London for getting these travel bargains. Just walk down Main Street. Many good deals are always posted in the windows of travel agents.

DRIVE WITHOUT A DRIVING LICENSE!

Another obscure "advantage" of Gibraltar is that although it is possible to get a driving license by examination or reciprocity, one does not technically need a driving license to operate an automobile there! The only other place we've come across with this interesting freedom is in the state of Alabama, USA. This doesn't mean you can race your Ferrari at top speed on the Gibraltar Freeway. Why? There are no freeways! Outside of the two-lane Main Street, there are a couple of one-lane roads cut into the mountain sides. Unless you want to meet your maker, you'd better be a skilled driver to negotiate these roads at more than 20 kph. There are signs prohibiting "learning drivers" from utilizing these roads. The rest of Gibraltar is a crowded little town about the size of Monaco (a bit over a mile square if you exclude the uninhabitable mountain slopes and military areas). There are policemen in traditional London Bobby garb on every street corner. It is faster to walk than drive through the populated parts of Gibraltar! The unpopulated mountain heights are a fortified military base off limits to the Gibraltar public. We suggest that you do not try to get insurance or rent a car without having a driving license. The ultra-polite Gibraltar policemen rarely impose fines but the Bobbies are very good at delivering stern warnings and military-style dressings down that are not easily ignored.

CONFIDENTIAL BANKING IN GIBRALTAR

Gibraltar, since the Spanish border was re-opened in 1985, has grown by leaps and bounds as an "offshore" financial center. It is very cheap (perhaps £300) to form a tax-free holding corporation through one of the many agents that provide such services. Of course, this £300 buys a barebones charter. All by itself it is a worthless piece of paper. You need, at minimum, a checking account, a registered office and a corporate secretary. The fixed annual duty to keep your company alive is £225. The annual running costs in lieu of taxes are the cheapest in Europe. Hong Kong is cheaper.

Banking secrecy is not perfect, but corporate accounts held in Gibraltar or elsewhere can make owners pretty well undiscoverable.

Because of the good communications with London and the proximity of over 500,000 British subjects residing in nearby Spain , who would rather not place their assets in Spanish controlled banks, Gibraltar-based British financial institutions are attracting many new customers every day. They provide all the usual services: portfolio management, credit cards, bill paying, checking or savings accounts in all currencies, safe deposit boxes, commodity and stock trading facilities. The quality of the services, in the author's opinion, is on about the same level as Jersey or Guernsey – that is to say, not nearly as good as in the exacting Swiss or Liechtenstein banks. But for unsophisticated dealings where regular foul ups or occasional failure to execute an order probably won't cost you a fortune, Gibraltar banks are adequate.

They are certainly suitable for mere savings accounts or holding mutual fund shares. For more technical or exacting services, you will need to operate through sharper and more responsible big city banks. In most "offshore" centers, top level people are competent but the locally recruited staff in Gibraltar, Cayman or Nauru are not up to the standards of Switzerland, London, Hong Kong. These places, with long banking traditions and fine educational systems are where the serious and smart money is.

British Sterling is the local currency, although you may from time to time catch a glimpse of the now rare Gibraltar pound. It is hardly used any more. Gibraltar money is pegged to British mainland currency on the basis of one for one.

In Gibraltar you can deal comfortably and reliably with anyone on this list of big league banks. You can write to any of them by their name and address, followed by "Gibraltar".

ALGEMENE BANK GIBRALTAR (owned by ABN Bank Netherlands), PO Box 100, 2-6 Main Street
BANK INDOSUEZ, PO Box 26, 206-210 Main Street
BARCLAYS BANK, 84-90 Main Street, Regal House, Queensway
HAMBROS BANK GIB LTD., PO Box 375, 32 Line Wall Road
LLOYDS BANK, 323 Main Street
ROYAL BANK OF SCOTLAND, 1 Corral Road
JYSKE BANK GIB LTD, PO Box 143, 76 Main Street

The number of chartered accountants (CPAs) in Gibraltar has nearly doubled since 1987 (12 to 23). There are now 21 banks where there were 10; 42 company management firms where there were 17. Money balances held in Gibraltar have quadrupled in the same period, although total deposits as of 1991 were only £4 billion.

Gibraltar is still far from the offshore big league. Its one clear "niche" at the moment is to finance, create and service offshore companies to hold title when foreigners buy a house. Property on the Spanish Costa Del Sol or on the coast of the Portuguese Algarve is typically owned by a Gibraltar corporation. At present, offshore financial services account for some 10 per cent of the colony's Gross National Product. The local government is hoping that this will expand to 35-40 per cent of GNP within the next 10 years. According to Labour prime minister Joe Bossano, "Our financial service industry is the fastest growing part of the economy".

In an effort to improve its tarnished image as a financial center, Gibraltar has set up a Financial Services Commission to protect the public from dishonesty, incompetence or malpractice by finance businesses registered in Gibraltar. The commission is producing regulations and licensing procedures for businesses including insurance brokers, professional trustees, company managers and investment dealers, brokers, managers and advisers. It is an offence for anyone in a new or existing business to operate without a license. Licenses will last for a maximum of three years but can be withdrawn or suspended. Supervision includes keeping accounts.

A full-time banking supervisor is responsible for building societies and bureaux de change, as well as banks. Six new banking licenses were granted in 1991 and the government wants to attract two or three more each year.

In the fiercely-competitive field of attracting investment funds, Gibraltar has an advantage in that its trust law is based on English common law, meaning asset protection trusts can spirit away funds from the grasping reaches of US lawyers and their clients. Asset protection trusts must be registered and have a corporate trustee. Other types of more-popular trusts do not have to be registered. All trusts with non-resident beneficiaries are exempt from Gibraltar tax on income from sources outside Gibraltar.

It is early days yet to see if this effort to solve Gibraltar's image problem will work and make its financial services more appealing to a wider audience. After the antics of Signal Life and Barlow Clowes, it is hardly reassuring that the Government has shied away from setting up a deposit protection scheme. For the time being, the potential investor should tread warily and take plenty of professional advice.

We recommend the annual *Gibraltar Financial Services Handbook* for a rundown on current legislation as well as a bundle of contacts and addresses. The book deals with finance, local laws, health, government and other material pertaining to Gibraltar living. Many ads and plenty of information. Priced right at currently £13 including postage and packing. Order from editor Diane Sloma, PO Box 555, Gibraltar.

GETTING THE BEST OUT OF LIFE IN GIBRALTAR

The type of people who live permanently in Gibraltar are not the wealthy *glitterati* of Monaco. For the most part, they are military and retired military personnel. The so-called "natives" are mainly individuals of Moroccan or Spanish descent whose ancestors were employed by the British Military. They learned perfect English. Now they are more British than the British ever were in their loyalty to the Queen, their craving for a full English breakfast (with kippers), afternoon cream tea, etc. The Gibraltarians hold down all the service jobs and are the shopkeepers. There is no group of independently wealthy big spenders as in Monaco. The one local casino is nowhere near as glitzy as Monaco or Baden-Baden. The few PTs who live permanently in Gibraltar are retired or semi-retired individuals who are (or were) in the financial services industry.

There is an abundance of lawyers, stock-brokers, real estate/insurance agents, turf accountants (bookmakers), travel agents, shipping and moving companies. Only one movie house operates. Other films and videos are shown in hotels and bars. Forget about legitimate theater, opera, live symphonic music or ''high level culture''. There are off-and-on little theater groups and, surprisingly, dozens of newspapers espousing all sorts of offbeat political views. Some ''newspapers'' are published on 8½in. X 11in. paper or what's called in Europe ''A4'' sheets. The daily *Chronicle*, a real newspaper ''Since 1801''', is a highly informative local rag with good apartment and job ads, local and international news, plus announcements of a large number of Church-sponsored social/religious activities.

Although there is no local university, a public library in addition to good primary and secondary schools (both public and parochial) seem to serve local needs.

Gibraltar has many pubs and a variety of fairly decent restaurants, some of which are awarded a government Heartbeat symbol to signify high standards. There are seven hotels in all price classes. White's Hotel (Holiday Inn) with rooms from £90 and The Rock, at about £50 a night, are just as good as hotels for triple the price in London. A solid English meal of tender roast beef, mashed potatoes, Yorkshire pudding, peas and carrots can be a welcome change from Spanish cuisine. Codfish simmered in olive oil and similar local dishes are what is waiting for you all over the Iberian peninsula. We soon tire of Spanish food. It is always drenched in olive oil.

For tourists, Gibraltar offers its own changing of the guard, mini-Buckingham Palace style. Every Tuesday at 10.20 am the ceremonial changing of the guard takes place in front of the Governor's residence, known as The Convent.

Although tiny, Gibraltar, at least from a distance, has a certain natural beauty. There is a breathtaking view to Africa from the top of the rock. Here, in the Upper Rock nature reserve you'll also find the rock apes. A tailless breed of monkey, they are the only monkeys living wild in Europe. Roaming freely, these friendly, charming creatures are Gibraltar's best-loved tourist attraction. Thousands of visitors on tour buses go to the Apes's Den to see them scampering among the pines and olive trees. The apes often "steal" cameras, sunglasses and shiny objects from surprised tourists.

There is a legend that "When the apes leave the Rock, the British will also go". Consequently, when their numbers dwindled during the Second World War, Sir Winston Churchill gave orders that their stock should never be allowed to fall below 35. This tradition has been strictly observed. Today the apes are the responsibility of the British Army. A member of the Gibraltar Regiment supervises the feeding and general well being of the apes.

Inside the Rock of Gibraltar you'll be able to take a tour of the man-made tunnels and natural caverns, including the famous St Michael's cave. It has been attractively converted into a large auditorium. Live entertainment can be seen and heard in a quite special atmosphere. A lower cave with its underground lake is a "must" for the day trippers.

Famous souvenirs are Gibraltar's coins and stamps, the latter being a big revenue earner as collectors worldwide subscribe to every new printing and get all stamps sent as first day issues.

YACHTS, CASINOS – IS THIS ANOTHER MONACO?

The Yacht Harbour is small when compared to the nearby deluxe Marina at Spain's Puerto Banus. Yet Gibraltar offers good yacht facilities, particularly for repairs, supplies and refurbishments. Gibraltar is a very popular place to register boats, both commercial shipping and yachts. Bareboat charters are available. But Gibraltar is not a place where the super rich live on multi-million dollar pleasure boats. There are many far nicer yacht harbours in Spain, Portugal, France and – yes – Monaco.

Although Gibraltar boasts a gambling casino with "live entertainment", it is just a piano and a singer, usually... Small potatoes! Nothing like Monaco's lively action with Las Vegas style shows and customers in tuxedos losing hundreds of thousands on the turn of a card. The Gibraltar action is decidedly "low roller". Much more gambling action is to be found across the border in the casinos of Spain's fashionable Marbella or Portugal's Estoril.

The Gibraltar Government Lottery is drawn every Monday. There is a weekly prize of £20,000. There are also two special lotteries per year, one in the summer for £75,000, while Christmas brings the grand prize of £100,000.

A unique experience when in Gibraltar is the laser show, dubbed the Gibraltar Laser Experience. It's a world first. Giant wall-size screen images and laser weapons portray exciting military-style action. The show is staged in caverns hewn during World War Two by defending soldiers deep inside the Rock of Gibraltar.

Spend £1 on a guided walking tour round the old Arab City Walls. Tours start every Friday at 10.30 am and tickets are available from the Tourist Office.

What else is there to do in the tiny colony?

Many things, according to the local tourist office. Marine sports, for example. For those with no previous experience diving lesson holidays with introductory courses are on offer. The courses are all taught by British Sub Aqua Club qualified instructors. They also offer boat diving for experienced divers. All necessary equipment is provided for participants.

The windsurfing school offers a wide variety of outdoor watersports. The school is based at Eastern Beach. Facilities include windsurfing, water-skiing, wave riders and pedalos. Pedalos (peddle boats for two) can also be hired at Sandy Bay and Catalan Bay. If they won't take you far enough, there are a number of boat cruises round the Bay. These set off from Waterport and are booked through local travel agents, who also peddle fishing cruises and dolphin safaris. There are many dolphins in the waters around Gibraltar. A special cruiser will take you out to see them. White whales and small sharks have also been sighted.

The average tourist stays in Gibraltar for no more than 48 hours.

HEALTH CARE: St Bernard's Hospital in Gibraltar was built to serve wartime military needs. Thus it is quite adequate in size for the current civilian community. If offers good quality care at reasonable prices to visitors with emergencies or "free service" to members of the local health plan/social insurance system. Health care will go high-tech when a new state-of-the-art hospital in the Europort-complex is finished. This private hospital will be the finest health care facility on the entire Iberian peninsula.

WATER: Obtaining a dependable supply of fresh water is a problem all over southern Spain due to periodic droughts. Gibraltar has elaborate systems to collect and store rainwater inside a catchment system that was started almost a thousand years ago when Gib Tarik (Tarik's Rock) first became an Arab fortress. The tap water system is safe to drink and provides a plentiful supply except during the worst droughts. Then British ships can (if necessary) supplement desalinization plant water with sweetwater supplies from England.

GIBRALTAR'S SECRETS: WHY THE BRITISH ARMY PAYS YOUR BILLS

Because it was always a military base and the civilian population and their needs have always been incidental, the expense of keeping Gibraltar well stocked with fuel, gasoline, foodstuffs, communication, etc is subsidised by the UK. Local costs often do not bear much relationship to the real costs involved. Gibraltar in many ways might be considered one big PX (Military Post Exchange). Military needs come first but locals get most of the benefits. Why? Because the civilian population exists mainly to service the military establishment. The civilians like existing arrangements; when a plebescite was held in 1986 about joining Spain, the vote was 12,000 to 44 against union with Spain.

As the last resident battalion of the army left in 1991, Gibraltar must find new jobs and create industries. Their target is a 12 per cent per annum growth rate, a somewhat optimistic figure. If attained it will put the country – growthwise – on a par with leaping South East Asia economies like that of Thailand. Will it happen? Will Gibraltar become a new Hong Kong?

Gibraltar politicians say new wealth will come from expanding tourism and financial services. The owner of the local taxi company, currently minister of Trade and Industry in the Gibraltar government, says that he envisages Gibraltar as the "future Hong Kong of Europe".

So far, Gibraltar is expanding fast as an offshore center. A vast, Danish sponsored, land reclamation project has created an immense bank of sand in the harbour on which a new office complex is being built (£17 per square foot). This **Europort Project**, as it is dubbed, will offer 80,000 square-meters of plush office space. It is largely finished but requires some finishing touches. A leisure complex is included, too, plus a hospital and 1,500 homes. The project is financed in part by the Danish Baltica group. A Scandinavian PT got the ball rolling. This chap, let's call him Larson, is currently living in Andorra but holds, among others, a Gibraltar passport. He can be seen driving his Mercedes 500SL around with American plates. Could "Larson" be our co-author? Shhhh...

GIBRALTAR, THE NEW HONG KONG?

Another PT-friend of ours – a Canadian named Garvin – recently moved from Gibraltar to Andorra. He does not believe the future for Gibraltar lies in the financial services sector. He writes this letter to us: "First: Gibraltar as 'financial center?' NEVER in this life or the next! To use a Sam Goldwynism: In two words: Im - possible. Some very slick and glib public-relations snow-job work is going on heralding Gibraltar as the new 'tax haven' and financial centre. It is not a tax haven, not even in the very limited Isle of Man sense. The laws are all there. But they don't always get applied very effeciently. Lots of people evade tax here, but I firmly believe that the Joe Bossano Socialist Government will work to correct that.

"It is now fashionable for capitalists to cuddle up to the socialists and 'ex'-communists and proclaim that they are not such bad guys and won't hurt us. There is no evidence of reformed ways other than world media bullshit. Bossano is benefiting from this. Fools think he will somehow let everybody play tax haven games on Gibraltar... As for the financial center dream: a) Gibbos haven't got the experience or skilled hands to run such a thing, b) Gibraltar communications are not nearly good enough even without the constant strikes and furthermore, witness the two-year long dispute of long distance phone operators or recent ongoing Gibtel/ C&W/TGWU three-cornered wrangle which nearly put a complete halt to all communications by wire or satellite out of Gibraltar. c) it is unlikely that the natives are going to change their basic negative attitude to hard work just to have a financial centre. The average Gibraltarian does not perceive any real benefits accruing to himself from the financial services sector. I think you would agree it takes foresight, planning, brains, determination and hard work to make some place a world-class financial centre. You must have skilled operators and a stable irrevocable legal structure, not something just cooked up by the outgoing government which was then replaced by socialists. Well, now, consider, the Gibraltarians have been subsidised by the UK since the 1700s. It hasn't yet come to an end, though the handwriting is on the wall. Why should a population suddenly decide to become PRODUCTIVE when it has never done nor had to do zip for two centuries plus? Up until two-three years ago the main employer was the British Admiralty, via H.M. Dockyard, which 'employed' 5,000 souls, some of whom were even honest enough to tell you they were paid basically for getting up in the morning. Honest! I was told this by dockyard workers when I slipped in my old MFV fishing-boat there as they lined up smoking hashish to watch my ladyfriend and myself hard at work scouring our ship's bottom. The Dockyard now privatised, is virtually bankrupt after £50 million refit expenditure. Workforce is down to 600 and they are still handing out redundancy notices!!! The Gibraltar population is accustomed to a free ride from the UK. They still mostly believe that situation can never change because of the 'crucial strategic importance' of Gibraltar. To the Gibbos this means, still, that if it were not for a British presence in Gibraltar the SPANISH would embargo the Straits of Gibraltar and not allow shipping to pass; I know that sounds loony but many of the old shellbacks who hold the real power in Gibraltar actually believe that. They think that the Spanish could really do it and that the sky would somehow fall if it happened.

"Further: Gibraltar BANKING is horribly inefficient, smug, obstructive and they just don't care. British banks are that way and it was British banks (Barclays, Lloyds) that taught the locals all they know and have the biggest foothold there. OK. Jyske Bank (DK) bought the one local private bank Gallianos but the staff is unchanged. All are unreconstructed locals. The most progressive banking element in Gibraltar at the moment is the SPANISH banks, if you could believe it. They are as everyone knows, hardly modern world-class financiers as yet. All those years of Franco petrification to overcome. Up until last year there was one tiny stock-broking firm on the Rock, Charles Stanley & Co. They were going nowhere and doing nothing. The one fellow they ever had who knew what he was doing (Roger Taylor) left and went into business for himself on the Costa. He is back in Gibraltar with Valmet. I did business with this firm and it was typically backward and small-town. Then James Capel & Co moved in, making it SOUND like the Big Guns had arrived; but HOW did James Capel go about it? Easy, they pinched Charles Stanley's latest green-as-grass office manager and best secretary. When I left Gibraltar THAT was the extent of James Capel & Co's presence on the Rock, just those two rattling around in a big building sold to James Capel & Co by Bassadones which used to occupy it and which made a killing selling cars (most lucrative business so far on the Rock as Gibraltarians are car-infatuated). James Capel's operation in Gibraltar is strictly an on-a-shoestring, do-it-cheap, just-in-case-something-actually-does-happen-here sort of thing. They will, I imagine, cut their losses and fade in a year or two if things fail to take off." [Hill's note: Capel did in fact abandon its Gibraltar office losing a bundle on its attempt to gain a toehold in a market that never materialised.]

"Believe me, Bill, the ATTITUDE, the INFRASTRUCTURE, the dependable communications and the skills are not there to make Gibraltar work as a financial centre. Right now Gibraltar is semi-succesfully selling something that hasn't actually happened at all but which they would like to see happen provided they don't have to do any work to make it go. It is a false facade. Same thing has happened with the tourist business. It has been 'decided' that since the Navy can't support the Rock any longer, tourism must do it. After the Frontier reopened, big tourism guns moved into Gibraltar full of optimism. Same big guns are now moving OUT of Gibraltar because as they say once people see it they refuse to come back again. Nobody with any taste recommends Gibraltar as a place for friends to live. It is filthy and Gibbos won't clean it up. It needs investment in plant and attractions. Locals won't spend a bean on those things. They want the returns of tourism without any investment and commitment."

So much for our pal and client Garvin. He is negative and has had nothing but bad experiences in Gibraltar.

He might, though, be carrying it a little bit too far, in this author's view. Granted, Gibraltar has some problems to overcome but also some advantages. It is definitely NOT a personal tax haven, although – as Garvin said – some people are quite succesfully slipping through the cracks, not paying a dime in tax. For corporations, however, Gibraltar is currently one of the best little havens in Europe. Gibraltar's rules are easy to comply with and very flexible, standing up to quite a few countries' anti-avoidance legislation provisions. Setting up a Gibraltar exempt-corporation can be done for very little money. Gibraltar is currently the ultimate European tax haven for corporations. The minute they change the rules, corporations can move to greener pastures with nothing more than a phone call.

As far as banking is concerned, we agree with Garvin. But instead of bitching, we will just find another "inn-keeper" for our deposits and trading. Today, we would probably plant one of our banking flags in Andorra. Or Luxembourg, London, New York or any other big banking centre with polite, efficient and knowledgeable staff. For non-serious money and current needs Gibraltar CAN be used. Just as residents of southern France use Monaco banks, the mother lode is naturally kept elsewhere, PT style. Whether the socialist government changes things will have to be seen. Currently, all newly formed exempt companies are given a 25-year tax holiday – a government guarantee of status quo. Thus, no drastic changes are to be expected unless the government does not want to honor its own guarantee. This, we might add, is NOT the British way. A word is a word is a word, especially when given in writing and given with the hand and seal of the local Royal Governor.

We feel no fear that things will change abruptly as far as company legislation is concerned. All companies are permitted to have in their statutes the so called "Cuba clause", enabling them to re-domicile if/when things get rough. The already very large number of companies (with some 90 to 100 new ones being incorporated every day) is too big a revenue-provider for government to change things now. Each year, every exempt company pays to Gibraltar government a flat rate tax of between £200 and £300. There are also indirect benefits to Gibraltar in terms of jobs that the offshore company "industry" has already created.

GETTING CHEAP WHEELS IN GIBRALTAR

Gibraltar is a good place for a PT to register his car. A car that has been owned a year on tourist plates can be registered tax free. One must have an address of record in Gibraltar. One is "officially" only supposed to be able to bring in and re-register an already used vehicle if it is part of personal belongings when taking up residence. So if some official starts asking questions, you'd better have your residence permit and a back-up story. Otherwise you may just have to forget about getting those tax free Gibraltar-plates. We understand that the government presently is quite generous with tax free plates. Car dealers and secretarial services will provide a local mailing address. The local office of the AA (British Automobile Association) will assist in all matters relating to car registration. It has all forms for a nominal fee. License plates that then stay with the car permanently are purchased locally at the cost of manufacture (a few pounds). These look like standard Great Britain plates but all start with the letter "G". A stick on decal for the backside of all Gibraltar-registered cars reads "GBZ". It is not "GBG" because Guernsey, Channel Islands, already has the "GBG" designation. The only cost for Gibraltar license plates is a small road tax of under £50 per year for most cars.

Registering a new car will involve paying a local tax of five per cent of the tax-free price but only if you are a non-resident of Gibraltar. You then get GG Plates or Gibraltar Tourist Registrations. If you reside in Gibraltar and purchase a new vehicle, you pay between 25 per cent and 35 per cent as customs duty on the sticker price. The rate of duty depends on the size of the engine.

WHERE TO FIND THE BEST CAR DEALS

Better deals on new cars can be found across the border, in Spain. There are several companies (car dealers) on the south coast operated by Scandinavian PTs. They have arranged deals to buy cars for the world's cheapest prices in Denmark. Their cars can then be picked up locally – in Spain. For tax minimization, they recommend the cars be kept on Danish tourist plates.

We have written a report on the subject, *The Free Car Report,* which you may order for £60 by mail from Scope International.

Our first choice in car dealers is International Car Trading, near Gibraltar. Ask for Michael or Ronald Foltinger, or Ms Alsira Pazos. The address is Auto Plaza, Ed Malambo Calle 5, Nueva Andalucia, 29600 Marbella, Malaga, Espana.

Michael and his father Ronald are Danish nationals. With their Spanish secretary Alsira, they operate just west of Marbella. Their company has been in business for many years. The team knows how to resolve even difficult situations and says "we will be delighted to welcome you any time". If you buy a car from them, let us know and we will send you a free report or something of interest. Get their price last! It will probably be the best deal around.

A similar car company specialising in reliable cheap cars with the cheapest auto RENTALS in Europe, "by the day, month or year", is located about an hour's drive from Gibraltar at the skyscraper vacation "village" of Fuengirola. It is easy to find, being in the huge

Hotel Pyr, right on the beach. Look for HELLE CAR RENTALS, Phone: 479800 or write c/o Hotel Pyr, Fuengirola, Malaga, Spain. Helle has a huge fleet of Spanish built Fiat Pandas for rent or sale. The Panda is one of the world's best and cheapest little cars. It is very well designed.

Another place to do comparison car shopping is: MONICAR, Plaza de la Iglesia 7-2 in the Spanish town of San Pedro de Alcantara, a few miles west of ultra-sophisticated Marbella. It is the local rep for Budget Rent-a-Car. Telephone-£ 789195.

Rental outfits always have low mileage cars for sale at discount prices. If you DO NOT expect to make Gibraltar your fiscal address, you can also buy your car tax free in Gibraltar on "GG" Gibraltar Tourist plates. But because of the dealer mark-up and no special discounts on factory list prices, base prices are at least 10 per cent more than in Denmark.

The only reason to buy and take delivery of a car in Gibraltar is: A) You don't want to make the trip to Denmark; B) You wanted immediate delivery in Gibraltar for some reason and could not wait the three weeks it would take for Danish Car Trading to get your special-order car from Copenhagen. There is also the possibility that one of the dealers in Gibraltar would have just the model you are looking for, at some sort of special price because it was a "demo" or a customer didn't pick it up and forfeited his deposit. Thus, when shopping for a car, it is always best to check with ten or twenty dealers. In Gibraltar, Fiat, Seat, Mazda and Renault-American Motors-Jeep are handled by ROCK MOTORS, PO Box 5, Phone: Gibraltar 78618, Telex GK 2277. There are a total of ten car dealers in Gibraltar. LUCAS-IMOSSI-FORD is one to remember. It also serves as the local office of the Auto Association. GEDIME MERCEDES is another name you might wish to know when you go car shopping. You don't need an address to write to these people. "Gibraltar" will do.

Finally, if you want my full report, *How to Own a New Luxury Car Every Year – Tax Free,* send $100 or £60 to Scope Books, 62 Murray Road, Waterlooville, Hants, PO8 9JL, Great Britain. I list many dealers and show you the way to buy low and sell high. Order form on last page of this book.

IS GIBRALTAR A SEX HAVEN?

One British reader, domiciled in Spain, writes to us about Gibraltar: "No sex in this place, Bill – zip, nada! But it is the best spot around for marriages. I got married in Gibraltar not so very long ago to a Spanish girl I had picked up in Spain. The procedure is extremely quick and simple. The officials involved are most polite, friendly and helpful. We arrived from Spain one day, were married the next morning and were away in the afternoon. Everything is done under British law. Talk to Mr Gracia, the Marriage Registrar, who is a very, very nice man and despite his Spanish name, is very English. Prior arrangements can be made by phone from anywhere in the world and can be made in your choice of either English or Spanish. I now have a Gib British Marriage Certificate. My local British consulate has all necessary papers and instructions."

This is good information for anyone in need of a quick "hitch". The rest of us, though, are more into good, clean and non-committing girlie fun. During my latest personal survey there didn't seem to be any massage parlors, girlie bars, strip shows, nor even any "Escort Services" advertised. No pleasure-peddling hostesses were to be found in the casino. With 15,000 servicemen stationed on Gibraltar, I found the lack of camp followers or working girls on the street a hard thing to believe. But perhaps I didn't know where to look.

There were no storefronts advertising cures for VD either but we did find one tattoo parlor. A total of three "joints" call themselves night-clubs: The Buccaneer, The Chimney Corner and Penelope's. There wasn't much happening at 10 pm. I didn't feel like propping up my eyelids with toothpicks to wait several hours to write a review of the late night action that was promised. More adventurous readers are invited to submit sexy experiences for the next edition. We will try to make updated reports more obscene. If there is anything of prurient interest to report, let me know. Probably local soldiers and sailors visit La Linea across the border in Spain. There, dark eyed flamenco dancers and fado singers help them find ecstasy or dirty blankets while unloading their wallets!

Two discos, Cornwall's in Cornwall's Lane and Reflections in the Caleta Palace hotel, cater to the under-20s. Here, a constant VERY LOUD pulsing beat summons you to a mirrored dance floor. There, at my age, 50, you are sure to get an unnerving headache. But you might enjoy watching the teeny-boppers jerking their cute little bodies through all sorts of jerky motions. Not that going there will help you score. Those gorgeous porcelain-skinned British/Gibraltar teenage girls are more interested in hip hopping to the latest hit singles than in paying any attention to dirty old men like us.

In Marbella, cruising the so-called Golden Mile coastal freeway at night guarantees you compliant company. The Golden Mile in daytime is the Spanish equivalent to Rodeo Drive. At night, however, it resembles Hollywood Hooker Boulevard. Most working ladies, however, are dreary, drug-dozed migrating birds from northern Europe. To check out local dolls, go to places like the Play Boy Club (San Pedro de Alcantara) or Maxims (Marbella Centro). Both places are standard hostess bars with the usual mixture of strip shows and $10 beers. Company is expensive too. Take them home for an hour of love – or reasonable facsimile – and plan on it setting you back more than $300! That's the asking price. On a slow night you can probably get two-thirds off.

Local girls who are usually too poor or too ugly to be found in bars are best picked up on the beaches or in parks. Just be friendly, smile and say "Hola!". That means "Hi". These girls do not expect to get paid for their services, although a few presents afterwards may well be in order. If you really DO wish to pay for sex, the entire Spanish coast (up to around Alicante) sports all sorts of kinky and not-so-kinky brothelbars, catering to all imaginable fantasies. Some of the bars are quite sleazy but others are, well... less sleazy. The girls often speak English, and some have extraordinary talent.

More on this subject in our special report, *Sex Havens*. For a grand selection of good looking, enthusiastic young bar girls, we recommend visiting neighboring Portugal. You'll get better value for money. As the sign outside says "Come Inside. Elefanto Branco Club. The most dip for your dollar."

More hot spots in Portugal are described in *Sex Havens*. But for those who cannot wait, we recommend that you sample the beauties of Hippotamus bar, just off the main Marques Pombal square in Lisbon, a five to six hour drive from Gibraltar. Worth the trip. So much for sex in southern Spain. Now we go back in history to...

GIBRALTAR'S BLOODY PAST AND PROBABLE FUTURE

Long before man ever thought of corporations or how to save inheritance taxes, people were inhabiting the rock of Gibraltar. Neanderthal man took up residence around 40,000 years ago, according to archaeologists. His successors lived and died leaving pots, arrowheads and tools behind. Then around 1500 BC, seatraders made camp on the Rock. Ancient Egyptians followed. Later came Phoenicians, who named Gibralter "Calpe", and Greeks. Around 200 BC, the

Romans arrived in the area. They held sway over southern Spain and Gibraltar and all of North Africa for 600 years. Then, as their empire crumbled, Vandals swept down destroying seven centuries of progress. Their cultural legacy was nil, except for the fact that they gave the southern Spanish region of Andalusia its name – a corruption of Vandalucia. They also gave the world "vandalism", a name for mindless destruction.

In 711 AD the Arab general Tarik ibn Zeyad conquered and claimed the Rock for Islam. Victorious Moors renamed the Rock Gibel-Tarik (meaning Tarik's Mountain). Over the centuries this has been softened to Gibraltar. They erected walls and defense towers which still stand.

When Spain first took Gibraltar in 1309 from the Moors, there was some difficulty in getting Spaniards to populate its not very hospitable confines. To overcome this prejudice the Spanish king set out a number of privileges to be earned by Spanish citizens taking on Gibraltar residence. There would be no taxes; for foreigners, residence for a year and a day on Gibraltar would confer Spanish citizenship; there would be no class distinctions, important in feudal times where what your father did for a living was exactly what you had to do, in Gibraltar one could be a free agent; thieves were forgiven and wives fleeing from their husbands were given sanctuary. As a result of these policies, Gibraltar soon became a cosmopolitan trade center and port.

Unfortunately, despite the comparatively liberal regime on Gibraltar, the Spanish were not to keep the Rock for long. Instead of using the money sent from the Spanish Government to build and strengthen fortifications, the corrupt Governor salted it away, with money he obtained by selling off the garrison's ammunition and stores. With the proceeds he built himself a splendid estate at Jerez, Spain. Inevitably, in 1333, Arabs struck again against Gibraltar's enfeebled defences. After a four month siege the garrison capitulated. The Moors were to stay for another hundred years until Spanish forces were once again able to evict them.

Spain held the Rock until 1704, when a force of Dutch, Germans and British took possession on behalf of Archduke Charles, the British-nominated claimant to the Spanish throne. For more than 50 years the border was sealed. Gibraltarians weren't allowed to take trips over the border to Spain. Spaniards were not allowed to set foot in Gibraltar upon penalty of death.

The fact that nearly all food and provisions had to come in by sea caused the British overlords to view the mostly Spanish and North African people stranded there as a natural resource to be exploited. All supplies had to be brought in by the Governor's monopoly contractor, who obtained inferior goods at the lowest possible prices. They were then sold on to locals with a mark up of 200 per cent or 300 per cent. Similar situations, albeit on a larger scale, can be found all over Africa today. Gibraltar's indigenous population was exploited in typical colonial fashion.

Another governor imposed a duty on wine and then, to ensure that his vinegar was sold, imposed a ban on the sale of beer.

Turning the screw a little further the same governor forbade the keeping of cows, sheep or pigs – so that his expensive, imported meat found a ready market.

This exploitation meant that most Gibraltarians were destined to stay very poor and dependant. Almost all were employees of the British military or small shopkeepers. The people were ready to introduce tax avoidance laws when finally given some autonomy after World War Two. Today, Gibraltar is a sanctuary for companies. Joe Bossano, the current leftist prime minister, recognises that the rest of the EC is not pleased with untaxed incomes finding an escape route via the Rock. He says "So what? Gibraltar produces nothing. All of our cash ends up being spent to profit the other countries of Europe". Spoken like a true intellectual with a firm grasp on political and economic reality.

Spain has made a number of recent attempts to reclaim sovereignty over Gibraltar. During the 1960s the Spanish Government progressively increased restrictions on travel and trade, finally sealing off the frontier with troops. A Spanish "Iron Curtain" went down in 1969. Before Spain's entry into the EC, to prevent a British veto on its membership, all frontier restrictions were lifted at midnight on 4 February 1985. This marked the starting day of Gibraltar's renaissance.

Gibraltar's defence and foreign policy is the responsibility of the British Government. The Queen of England appoints a Royal Governor as the representative of the Crown. However, Gibraltar is self-governing with regard to domestic matters. The present Legislature consists of the Governor and the Gibraltar House of Assembly founded in 1969.

Commerce and trade since 1985 has flourished in this hospitable environment. **Gibraltar is a member of the European Community** – unlike Jersey, Guernsey, Sark and the Isle of

Man. This came to pass as a result of Paragraph (4) of Article 227 of the EC Treaty. This Article provides that the Treaty shall, with certain exceptions, apply to "European territories for whose external relations a Member State is responsible". The UK is such a member state. Gibraltar must thus comply with Community general directives and regulations. Unlike the Channel Islands, it was not made an exception.

Gibraltar's special circumstances were recognised at the time of the UK's accession to the EC but Article 28 of the Act of Accession only temporarily relieves Gibraltar from compliance with Community rules on: 1) The Common Customs Tariff; 2) The Common Agricultural Policy; 3) Harmonisation of Turnover Taxes – notably VAT.

Future EC Directives will have to be implemented by the Gibraltar Government and incorporated into domestic legislation. The widespread talk of a pan-European harmonisation of withholding taxes on bank account interests has thus scared some depositors away from Gibraltar (and fellow EC-member Luxembourg). Most Gibraltar citizens would view any withholding schemes as diabolical thievery. There is bound to be years of squabbling. We predict that the tax haven days of Gibraltar are numbered. Want us to pick a date for the party to end? How about 2020? Your guess is as good as ours. But for at least ten or 20 years more, the tax avoidance possibilities will allow Gibraltar to remain an excellent base for offshore corporations.

HOW TO SET UP YOUR OWN OFFSHORE TAX-HAVEN CORPORATION ON GIBRALTAR

Beginning in 1967, a series of laws were passed to make Gibraltar an attractive tax haven. This legislation concerned the establishment of tax-exempt companies. Gibraltar tax-exempt companies can be incorporated in Gibraltar or they can be companies incorporated abroad but registered on Gibraltar. The latter are called non-resident companies.

In either case, exempt companies pay a flat rate annual tax regardless of the gross receipts or level of profit made. If "ordinarily resident", the fixed tax is £225 per annum and the fee or tax is £200 if not so resident. The registered Gibraltar branch of an overseas company pays £300 per annum. Naturally, high-tax countries do not like to see "their" corporations or taxpayers move elsewhere. Thus, they pass what is known as anti-avoidance legislation. A number of countries have introduced local laws stating that all capital gains arising from the sales of shares of foreign companies owned by locals will be taxed at a confiscatory rate at home if the company in question didn't pay any income tax where it was registered (ie, Gibraltar). This move prompted tax planners like us to set up local companies in places such as the Antilles, where a tax of a few percentage points is in force. Naturally, the high-tax countries still viewed this as abuse. But it worked for a few years until this loophole was closed. How? Britain and a few other countries passed laws that require locally-owned offshore corporations wherever they may be, to pay a tax amounting to at least 50 per cent of the tax they would have paid if they were British registered limited companies. This rule, naturally, was passed to make the use of offshore-companies in low or no-tax jurisdictions look unattractive. To circumvent London, Gibraltar acted swiftly. In 1983, the Income Tax (Qualifying Companies) Rules were passed, stating that qualifying companies are chargeable to tax on their profits at the rate of two per cent on income not remitted to Gibraltar and 17 per cent on income so remitted. With this law and a bit of planning, one can effectively set one's own income tax rate up to 17 per cent. This is more than 51 per cent of the basic corporate tax of 25 per cent a taxpayer would have had to pay if he stayed a British limited company. This manoeuvre allows a corporation to set its own tax at 50 per cent of the UK rate. Gibraltar is delighted to have its exempt corporations stand in line for the right to pay taxes.

With this creative 1983 law, Gibraltar became the first corporate tax haven where one could actually pay a flexible tax in order to save taxes. Obviously, it is a great deal for Gibraltar to have corporations wanting to pay 50 per cent of the British tax in order to escape the full British tax.

Relatively few companies, however, play this game, since most stockholders prefer to remain anonymous beneficial owners of exempt companies – exempt, that is, from all taxes but the £225 annual fee.

It is extremely easy to incorporate a company in Gibraltar. You need two subscribers and a registered office, ie a mail drop, on the Rock. To register an exempt company, application must be made to the Financial and Development Secretary. The company must also have paid-up capital of at least £100 or equivalent in another currency.

One of Scope's consultants can put your entire set-up together. He will provide nominee stockholders and the two subscribers, thus keeping your name (which he does not have to know, by the way) off the public records. Nominee directors who will do your bidding (two) are provided, with a prestigious registered office address in downtown Gibraltar. The client alone controls all funds. Contact Scope if you require a Gibraltar offshore corporation guidance service. The initial fee includes full information, all required corporate documents, opening of functioning bank accounts in the name of the company and full advisory service. The annual all-inclusive cost after set-up is either £650 or US $1,000. For less than full services, the fee can be reduced. The main requirement for exempt status is that no Gibraltarian or Gibraltar resident has a beneficial interest in the shares of the company and that the company does not trade or carry on business in Gibraltar. It can trade or carry on business with other Gibraltar-exempt companies. The company can use its office premises in Gibraltar for the purposes of re-invoicing, transfer trades, transacting any business with non-residents or with other exempt or qualifying companies. There are no other restrictions on the appointment of directors or officers of an exempt company. Meetings may be held in or outside of Gibraltar, thus allowing the company to be managed and controlled locally. A secrecy provision in the Ordinance prevents the disclosure of details concerning the beneficial owners of the company.

REGISTERING YOUR YACHT, AIRCRAFT OR EXPENSIVE CAR

All ships registered in Gibraltar are registered as British ships under Part 1 of the United Kingdom Merchant Shipping Act 1894. Similar rules govern aircraft and cars. Gibraltar is part of the British registry. All documentation is therefore **identical** to that in the UK, although registering in Gibraltar has many advantages over mainland United Kingdom. First, a person of any nationality can arrange for a craft to be registered under the ownership of a Gibraltar exempt company. In addition to benefiting from the tax concessions, the vessel can fly the British Red Ensign and enjoy the privileges and protection of the British flag. Secondly, there is no VAT. Other benefits include: no import duty if the boat is not based in Gibraltar; no annual tonnage tax as in most countries; no taxes on the sale of the boat or on the sale of the company shares.

GIBRALTAR'S POLITICAL STATUS

The official population of Gibraltar is about 31,000. Thus the population is almost exactly the same as Monaco's. There the similarity ends. Monegasques and Gibraltarians are totally different breeds.

The civilian population was entirely evacuated to Great Britain and other safe locations in the Commonwealth during World War II. Gibraltar, with Malta, played a vital strategic role from 1940 to 1945 in denying Axis Powers the use of the Mediterranean. Gibraltar is the gateway to the Atlantic. For those unaware of the historical importance of Gibraltar, it should be noted that even 200 years ago, big guns mounted on Gibraltar could destroy any ship passing between the Mediterranean Sea and the Atlantic Ocean. Guns and missiles on Gibraltar still control access to the Mediterranean.

Occupation of Gibraltar, combined with control over the Suez Canal, kept the Mediterranean a British lake for centuries. Gibraltar, with its thousands of square feet of still secret military installations tunnelled over the centuries deep into the bomb-proof Rock remains an important air/sea base. Even today, with its airport and fortifications, Gibralter is still the most strategic asset of NATO.

With the Spanish commitment to NATO running from lukewarm to cold and back again, but always less than complete, we feel that Gibraltar will remain British, at least during our lifetime. It is too important a chunk of real estate to be handed over to Spain, a country that periodically tilts between monarchy, anarchy, communism, fascism and fragmentation. Because of the long Arab occupation of Spain (or for whatever reason may be your personal favorite), the Spaniards are an over-emotional, often irrational people. Far more than their European brothers they indulge in miliary coups, self-flagellation and religious excess. Their national sport involves the ritual blood sacrifice of bulls by effeminate slender young men. These toreadors are national heroes, getting paid more than movie stars for their efforts in killing a dumb, brute animal every Sunday.

Corruption levels are high, inefficiency in all things is great. Siestas and putting things off for manana are in contrast to Anglo traditions of "getting the job done right!". Spain is modernizing and changing its ways, but like Turkey and Greece (also Arab dominated for centuries), the Spanish people don't think like mainstream Europeans. Their super-catholic intolerance of divergent customs, religions and morality also leaves something to be desired.

For those who like the area and climate, the choice as we see it is:

1) To go native 100 per cent in Spain,
2) To have a "vacation" home or apartment in Spain with finances handled and shopping to be done in Gibraltar, or
3) To live in and do everything from Gibraltar.

We feel that number two is the preferred option. Why?

OWNING A HOME IN NEXT-DOOR SPAIN – PROS AND CONS

Our personal view is that the greater recreational facilities and lower costs of Spain make owning or renting there a better bet. If one is actually going to spend a lot of time in the area, the beaches, diversions, fine golf, huge variety of cosmopolitan activities, affluence and entertainment in a place like Marbella makes Gibraltar look pretty tatty. If one wants to rent a deluxe villa with pool, tennis courts, sea-view and well-kept garden – it is just impossible in Gibraltar. But thousands of such bargain paradises exist for holiday rentals or purchase just a few miles away in Spain. During the winter "off season" many British pensioners rent lovely apartments on the Costa del Sol for less money than it costs to pay just their heating bills back in Edinburgh or London.

Periodic visits or even phone calls or mail to Gibraltar can handle shopping and investments. Gibraltar shopping, banking, and boat and car registration are easy to manage. Most savvy foreigners used to form a Gibraltar-exempt company to hold title to their Spanish residential properties. As tenants rather than owners they felt safer from lawsuits, confiscations or tax claims. Now, however, Spain has put an end to this practice with a new law popularly referred to as the Anti-Gibraltar law. Real estate owned by foreign companies will have to pay an annual tax of three to five per cent of property value, roughly half a million pesetas on the average Spanish house. Only companies domiciled in countries with which Spain has entered into double taxation treaties can avoid this. So today, foreigners do business as usual but use a non-resident Irish company as the owner of the property instead of a Gibraltar company. These are suitable for the same purpose, Ireland, as an EC member, has a wide net of double taxation treaties.

When living in nearby Spain, Gibraltar may be used as a transport gateway when coming to or going from the area by sea or air. Auto ferries between Morocco, Italy and England are priced similarly whether boarded in Gibraltar, Spain or Portugal. Air travel via Gibraltar can be 50 per cent below the cost of similar trips starting in Spain or Portugal.

The only reason for owning property or actually living full time in Gibraltar would be that you run a financial-services business. Then, having a Gibraltar office and home address would save the trouble of learning Spanish (to take tests and be in compliance with unfamiliar Spanish laws). Of course, as in most British colonies, five years of residence makes you a citizen. A Gibraltarian has a choice of a Gibraltar passport with essentially the same rights. The only difference is that a Gibraltarian gets special preference as to local rent-controlled housing and first rights of refusal on the rental or sale of certain publicly-owned real estate. But if Gibraltar did some day become Spanish, the Gibraltarian then would automatically become Spanish.

We have always advised PTs to stay away from ownership of property except perhaps in tax havens. As to residential property in Spain, owned by offshore corporations - formed in Gibraltar or anywhere else - now they will attract a considerably higher annual tax than individually-owned property. The offshore company owning Spanish property now must file tax returns annually in Spain and pay a hefty one-third tax on the **imputed** or fair rental income, even if the property is vacant or given free to a "caretaker". The Spanish tax collector knows that the caretaker is usually the same person who secretly owns the offshore corporation. Thus the old justification for offshore corporate ownership ie the tax savings of about ten per cent on property transfers, which do not show up if corporate shares rather than property are transferred, is no longer cost-effective. Local property taxes, water and electricity costs in popular tourist traps have been raised as much as 100 times their level of five years ago, regardless of how title is held.

Further it is said that the *Hacienda* or Spanish tax collector has initiated a get-tough policy on foreigners who live more than six months each year in Spain and do not pay taxes on their worldwide income. They find such "delinquents" by requiring a Spanish "fiscal number" for obtaining a telephone line, electricity, gas, garbage collections, a bank account, a local credit card, or even making contracts of any sort in Spain. To get a fiscal number, you must fill out a form and tell the tax collector your life story.

These new tax policies have driven a large percentage of foreign property owners to liquidate their properties at any price, or even to abandon properties with loans on them. Prices on villas in Spain are down as much as 90 per cent from just a few years ago. The Spanish are apparently shooting themselves in the foot just as the French did two decades ago with similar policies. The result in Spain is the same as it was in France, a massive outflow of wealthy foreigners with local middle class Spanish buyers picking up property at well below cost. **Maybe this is what the local politicians want.** Seduce rich foreigners into making investments, then confiscate.

Buying a property in Portugal through a Gibralter-based offshore company still carries substantial tax advantages and this may be a viable alternative to falling into the clutches of the Spanish authorities.

A PT doesn't buy real property outside of tax havens except in very special situations:

1. The price has to be a steal;
2. The property should be acquired with "no money down";
3. Title normally should be kept in a pen-name for whom the PT has obtained a banking passport;
4. Any loans or debts (like taxes) on the property should be uncollectable from the PT personally;
5. Offshore corporations, foundations, trusts and such should never be used because they require paperwork and annual reports that put you under the control of lawyers, accountants and governemnt bureau-rats who should know absolutely nothing about you or your activities;
6. The PT's creed -**If you can sleep in it, on it or with it, rent it**

SHOULD YOU GET A GIBRALTAR PASSPORT?

A true PT does not obtain any residence permits, nor does he want work permits or any other bits of government paper. These might put him in the maw of those information-swapping, tax-bill spewing Big Brother computers. But just for the record. as of 1991, obtaining a residence permit in Gibraltar is pretty straightforward. As Gibraltar is part of the EC, EC nationals cannot be refused a residence permit nor a work permit, although the Immigration Ordinance states that ''undesirable persons may be refused a residence permit or have one revoked in the interest of public policy, security or health''.

Most non-EC nationals can also get a residence permit. You (as a non-EC person) will have trouble obtaining a work permit unless:

1) There is a genuine vacancy for which there is no Gibraltarian available, AND;
2) The employer will undertake to repatriate the worker (you) if and when your services are no longer required, AND;
3) Acceptable arrangements for local accommodation are made (meaning that they do not want you sleeping in a cardboard box in their already crammed streets).

Arranging for a ''permanent domicile address'' in Gibraltar might be a good idea under some circumstances. We are working on finding a service similar to the reliable and efficient agency we have in Sark. Any recommendations on this subject will be gratefully received. Because Gibraltar (unlike Sark) is in the European Community, it will perhaps one day be subject to strict tax enforcement and all the usual Big Brother tax-information swapping deals. If that happens we would lean even more towards Sark for serious banking and as our offshore domicile and fiscal address.

APPENDIX: USEFUL ADDRESSES

Note: The international area code for Gibraltar is 350.

AA (International Driving Licenses)

Gibraltar Travel Ltd, 15 Irish Town, Gibraltar. Tel: 73550

Gibraltar Bankers Association, PO Box 557, Neptune House, Marina Bay, Gibraltar. Tel: 79374, fax: 75684

Avis Rent-A-Car, 15 Bayside Road, Gibraltar. Tel: 75552, fax: 76189

British Car Rentals, 20 Line Wall Road, Gibraltar. Tel: 70514

Budget Rent-A-Car, PO Box 327, 5 Queensway, Gibraltar. Tel: 79666

Europcar – Godfrey Davis, 21 Horse Barrack Lane, Gibraltar. Tel: 76520

Ford Rentacar, 33 Waterport Circle, Gibraltar. Tel: 75627, fax 79410

Gibraltar Chamber of Commerce, PO Box 27, Suite 11, Don House, 30/38 Main Street, Gibraltar. Tel: 78376, fax: 78403

Immigration Office, Waterport, Gibraltar. Tel: 71453

Passport Office, Convent Place, Gibraltar. Tel: 70071

ACCOUNTANTS IN GIBRALTAR

L P Bruzon & Co, Suite 33, Victoria House, 26 Main Street

Carboni Jardim & Co, 4 Governors Lane. Tel: 79033

Clement & Co, Haven Court, 5 Library Ramp. Tel: 74051

Dennis M Clinton, PO Box 480, 34 Engineer Lane. Tel: 76679

Clintons, PO Box 239, Suite 2, Gibraltar Heights

Coopers & Lybrand, 1 Corral Road. Tel: 78777

Durante & Co, PO Box 256, 45 City Mill Lane. Tel: 73330

Ernst & Young, Suite 5, International House, Bell Lane

Estella & Co, Suite 23, 2nd Floor, Victoria House, 26 Main Street

Charles Frieze & Co, PO Box 46, 5 Cannon Lane. Tel: 79918

Halpern & Woolf, Halpern House, 79 Prince Edwards Road

PWI/Hassan & Co, Suite 9/4, Int. Comm. Centre, Casemates

Moore Stephens, Suite 34, Victoria House, 26 Main Street

G A Olivera & Co, Suite 4, 4 Giros Passage. Tel: 77122

Olivero & Dodwell, PO Box 417, 12/3 Georges Lane. Tel: 78440

Pannell Kerr Forster, Suite 32, Victoria House, 26 Main Street

KPMG Peat Marwick, Suite 12, Gibraltar Heights. Tel: 74015

Ravenscroft & Co, Suite 204, Neptune House, Marina Bay P.C.

Roberts & Co, Suite 215B, Neptune House, Marina Bay

Spicer & Oppenheim, 10th fl., Int. Comm. Centre Casemates Sq.

Thorogood & Co., 120 Main Street. Tel: 76344

LAWYERS IN GIBRALTAR

Attias & Levy, Suite 3, 3 Irish Place - Tel: 72150

J I Azzopardi, PO Box 510, Suite 14, The Water Gardens 2

H K Budhrani, 62/1 Main Street - Tel: 73521

L W G J Culatto, Mews House, Horse Barrack Lane - Tel: 74096

W J Edwards, PO Box 452, 3 Parliament Lane - Tel: 76517

E C Ellul, Suite 10, Gibraltar Heights - Tel: 70921

Finch & Partners, 3 Governor's Parade - Tel: 76363

Fox & Gibbons, Hadfield House, Library Street - Tel: 77750

Charles A Gomez, 15a Tuckeys Lane - Tel: 74998

Glaisyers, PO Box 451, 3/1A Parliament Lane - Tel: 76517

J A Hassan & Partners, PO Box 199, 57/63 Line Wall Road

A J Haynes, 12/1 Bell Lane - Tel: 74261

Isola & Isola, 3 Bell Lane - Tel: 78363

John Ross Jones & Partners, Suite 21, Victoria Hs, 26 Main Street

A Lombard, Suite 1, Haven Court, 5 Library Ramp - Tel: 71987

Marrache & Co, PO Box 85, 5 Cannon Lane - Tel: 79918

P X Nunez, 123 Main Street - Tel: 77554

L R Peralta, Suite 5, Gibraltar Heights - Tel: 76172

J B Perez, 4/4 Giros Passage - Tel: 76222

J J Rosado, 62 Main Street - Tel: 71959

E M Russo, 12B College Lane - Tel: 78437

Stagnetto & Co, 186 Main Street - Tel: 73530

W Triay Louis & Partner, PO Box 147, Suite 1, Gibraltar Heights

Triay & Triay, PO Box 15, 28 Irish Town - Tel: 72020

Vasquez Benady & Co, Cloister Hs, Fountain Ramp - Tel: 76108

B Vaughan, 120 Main Street - Tel: 78270/79887

BEST NEWSPAPER IN GIBRALTAR

If you are considering moving to Gibraltar, the local paper is a good outlet for advertising your skills or services. Look for rentals or send in your ad seeking a place to live. We suggest that you subscribe to the *Gibraltar Chronicle* before you actually move to Gibraltar. Before your arrival you'll be familiar with the place. You'll know exactly what is going on! A personal love ad might even put you in touch with a terrific girlfriend (or mate).

The Gibraltar Chronicle

2 Library Ramp, Gibraltar

Tel: 78597, telex: GTIAGY 2205 GK, fax: 79927

WHERE TO STAY IN GIBRALTAR – HOTELS:

Bristol (two star),

Cathedral Square.

Tel:76800, fax: 77613

Bright white building and a charming restaurant reached by a covered bridge across from a narrow side street, nice garden.

Caleta Palace (three star),

Catalan Bay.

Tel: 76501, fax: 71050/42143

Holiday hotel, built out on the rocks over the sea with sun terraces and a swimming pool with steps down to the water. Most rooms have balconies overlooking sea. In the Caleta Palace you will find the **Reflexions** disco. There, the teenagers of Gibraltar hang out. Especially lively on Friday nights, after 11 pm.

Continental

1 Engineer Lane.

Tel: 76900, fax: 41702

Small, centrally situated but without a restaurant, inexpensive.

Gibraltar Beach Apartment Hotel

Sandy Bay.

Tel: 76191

Clean place, wonderful sunsets, inexpensive. Units have direct access to the sands and the crystal-clear Mediterranean. A super love nest.

White's Hotel (Holiday Inn) (four star)

Governors Parade.

Tel: 70500, fax: 70243

One of the most modern places in town. This hotel has an outdoor supervised parking lot right in front of the hotel! Convenient parking near the center of town is a rare find in Gibraltar.

Ocean Heights Apartment Hotel

Montague Place.

Tel: 75548

Centrally located in town, two minutes from Main Street and close to the harbor. Choose between studios, one two or three bedroom units. Cheaper than a regular hotel and better for a long term stay. Reserve in advance!

Queens (two star)

1 Boyd Street.

Tel: 74000, fax: 40030

A rather plain, tall building. Furnishings are very Spanish, Rough plaster walls, dark wood beams in the bar. Elegant dining room.

The Rock Hotel (four star)

Europa Road.

Tel: 73000, fax: 73513

Set in beautiful nine-acre grounds on the Rock's sunny western side with magnificent views of Spain and North Africa. This is the place for the traditionalist. There are gentle walks through the geranium gardens, as well as a wisteria-covered terrace for a sundowner. Deadly bar.

Sunrise Motel

Devil's Tower Road.

Tel: 41265, fax: 41245

Modern motel, five minutes from the frontier and airport and two minutes walk from Eastern Beach.

INVESTMENT MANAGERS AND FINANCIAL CONSULTANTS

There are many investment and financial consultants who have been able to perform their services free from government regulations. The absence of regulatory controls and legislation always attracts cowboys, dubious sharepushers and shady types! How this situation will change with the new Financial Services Commission has yet to be seen.

Thousands of people lost millions due to their misplaced confidence in Barlow Clowes which was operating out of Gibraltar until a few years ago. We warned all of our personal consulting clients against doing business with this firm.

This list of investment consultants is in NO way meant to be our stamp of approval. We are NOT recommending any one here – nor are we saying they are no good either.

Barclaytrust Gibraltar Ltd., 17 Market Lane

GM Benady & Co, PO Box 240, 4 Irish Place

Castiel Winser Financial Consultants Ltd, 3/1 City Mill Lane

CMI Group Service Ltd, Suite 42, Victoria House, 26 Main Street

Dominion International Ltd, Suite 2, Int. House, Bell Lane

Bernard T Down & Co, 104-106 Irish Town

Eagle Star Services Ltd, PO Box 517, 209 Main Street

Eurofile Fund Managers Ltd, 3B Rosia Road

Fiduciary Trust Ltd, Suite 3 15 Horse Barrack Court

Financial Direction Ltd, PO Box 166, 1 Irish Place

First Continental Ltd, Suite 22, Don House, 30/38 Main Street

Garson Ltd, Suite 31, Don House, 30/38 Main Street

Gibraltar Asset Management Ltd, PO Box 166, 1 Irish Place

Gibraltar & Iberian Trust Co Ltd, 21 Cannon Lane

Hill Samuel Int SA, PO Box 619, 2/f 6 Engineer Lane

HPL Financial Services Ltd, PO Box 16, 234 Main Street

Key City Investment Trust Ltd, 4 Irish Place

Kingsley Hay Financial Services Ltd, 120 Main Street

Labrow International Group, Suite 44, Victoria House

Laurentian Ltd, Suite 21, Don House, 30/38 Main Street

Lindsay Duncan (Iberia) Ltd, 28 Irish Town

London Portfolio Services Plc, 101 Neptune House Marina Bay

Malmstrom & Valdemarsson Ltd,2B-1 Cazes Arcade, 143/145 Main St

MIM Britannia Int Ltd, Suite 206, Neptune House, Marina Bay

Ocean Finance Ltd, Suite 44 Victoria House, 26 Main Street

Opepas, PO Box 199, 57/63 Line Wall Road

Riggs Valmet Ltd, 108-111 Neptune House, Marina Bay

Savignon Insurance Brokers Ltd, 315 Main Street,

The Orion Group, PO Box 503

All the banks, listed elsewhere in this report, also do investment and portfolio management for private clients.

The government regulatory offices are The Financial Development Secretary, Treasury Building, Secretary's Lane, Gibraltar, tel: 76620, fax: 79901; and The Financial Services Commission, Suite 5B, 50 Town Range, Gibraltar, tel: 40283, fax: 40282.

Note: Once again, we do not vouch for the integrity of any particular advisors. Use at your own risk. All readers should note that our special advisory service should be considered before entering into ANY business with Gibraltar investment managers or financial consultants. Some are OK but readers are known to have had costly experiences with others.

We are not saying that Gibraltar needs financial policemen and a USA-style straitjacket legislative framework to regulate every move in the financial services industry. The Rock may well have only one financial scandal per year – a modest number compared to the more frequent follies of London, New York or Tokyo – but one in such a small town is too many. Especially when **you are the one** being left holding an empty bag. Beware! Beware! Beware!

MOROCCAN ENCLAVES CEUTA AND MELILLA

[This special section has been contributed by Adam Starchild, author of many books and articles including Scope's *The Tax Haven Report.*]

Two very small Spanish enclaves on the coast of Morocco are practically unknown but may be appealing to some PTs. Ceuta and Melilla are Spanish cities and although Spanish taxes apply, the rates are only half those imposed in mainland Spain. Both cities are completely duty-free ports as well, making them particularly useful bases for a PT keeping a yacht on the Mediterranean and not spending long enough on land to be deemed resident by the Spanish tax authorities. There is also no VAT.

On the other hand, there can be advantages to becoming a legal resident of one of the enclaves, since the cost of maintaining an apartment is low and provides a visible tax residence to satsify the authorities in jurisdictions with higher taxes. Since the enclave is your declared legal residence and you are voluntarily paying Spanish taxes - admittedly at a 50 per cent discount - nobody is monitoring where you spend your time. As a Spanish resident, you are entitled to use your town house in Madrid for business visits, perhaps five days a week, or spend time in your vacation villa in the Canary Islands. The enclave address on your tax return and your residence card is what gets you the tax break, not your physical presence.

Citizens of EC countries can establish residence automatically since Spain is a member of the EC. All Spanish double taxation treaties apply so, to your home country authorities, you are not residing in a tax haven.

Between 1497 and 1848, Spain acquired two enclave cities and three garrison enclaves on the coast of North Africa, with a combined area of 14 square miles. According to the Spaniards, this area, with over 200,000 Spanish citizens, represents a legal part of metropolitan Spain.

Ceuta and Melilla have about 80,000 people each. In addition to the large civilian population, there are sizeable garrisons.

On the Mediterranean side of the Strait of Gibraltar, the cities are situated between 35 and 36 degrees north. This places them roughly on the same latitude as Memphis in the United States, Tokyo in Japan, and Malta, Crete and Cyprus. They have a mild sub-tropical climate with summer drought and winter rain.

The city of Ceuta is directly across the Strait of Gibraltar, 12 nautical miles south of the Rock. Mount Hacho, a 636 feet high mountain on the eastern extreme end of the cape, which is one mile east of the center of Ceuta, formed the African side of the ancient world's Pillars of Hercules.

On a large cape which juts out 15 miles from the coast, Melilla is 155 nautical miles east of Ceuta. An overnight ferry runs between the two enclaves weekly. Land connection is by Morocco's route P-39, a distance of about 190 miles. Much of it is winding mountain road, so a trip by car takes about nine hours.

Melilla airport has approximately five flights daily to Malaga on the mainland, while Ceuta has a military heliport. Tangier airport has connecting fights to Casablanca, Madrid, Malaga, and Paris. Frequent ferry services link Ceuta with Algeciras, Spain, and a daily round trip connects Melilla with Malaga.

Ceuta has an area of nine square miles, while Melilla is four square miles, these compare with the 2.4 square miles of Gibraltar.

The population split of each enclave is about 80 per cent Spanish and 20 per cent Moroccan. This Moroccan percentage, however, can be a bit misleading, however, as it refers to actual population. Between 8,000 and 10,000 Morrocans cross the border daily from the surrounding countryside either to work or shop. There are also sevral hundred shop owners from India in the enclaves, although that is still less than one per cent of the population but Indian commercial influence in the duty-free shopping industry is significant.

In practice, there is little concern shown by the Spanish border authorities to inspect anything carried into Ceuta either personally or by car. On the other hand, Moroccan customs police frequently strip-search young European backpackers as they leave Morocco for Ceuta, on the assumption that they may be carrying drugs. The arrest rate on the Moroccan side has been fairly high.

Ceuta has a civil government and the city is administered as a municipality of Cadiz Province, while Melilla is administered by Malaga Province. But the cities also have a special status in that they each have one Deputy and two Senators in the Spanish Parliament. For practical purposes, the city administration is the government and there are no functions for the provincial government to carry out.

Ceuta has an excellent natural harbor and is nearly as busy as Bilbao on the Spanish mainland. This isn't some quiet backwater but a booming freeport which can be a useful and inconspicuous base for a PT. Melilla port is also modern but considrably smaller than Ceuta.

Upon entering the port, Ceuta appears to have many more tall, new buildings than Melilla, which gives the city a more modern look.

There is much more useable pier space in Ceuta than in Melilla because much of Melilla's inner harbor is taken up by its beautiful recreational beach.

Ceuta's location at the busy strait contributes greatly to its traffic, whereas Melilla has fewer visitors than those directly destined for the port itself. For a PT yachtsman, this gives some edge to Ceuta for an ability to disappear in the crowd. Melilla is known for its excellent seafood, and has a small fishing fleet. The port facility at Ceuta has many sport and recreation boats, rows and rows of pleasure craft, compared to a fairly small nautical club at Melilla used mainly by small sailing craft.

Ceuta is only a one-hour ferry ride from Algeciras and since it is a shorter journey than the Algeciras-Tangier connection, the port rivals Tangier as an easy entry to Morocco from Spain. The ferries carry both passengers and vehicles on at least eight round trips daily, rising to 15 scheduled crossings in the tourist season. Ceuta newspapers cover happenings across the Strait in the towns around Algeciras and there is close contact with the area for entertainment and visiting. Melilla is much less accessible than Ceuta. A daily ferry connects the city to Malaga, eight hours away.

Since the mid-1960s, Ceuta has been designated a duty-free port of entry for Apin. There are about 500 small appliance stores in Ceuta, selling radios, stereos, cameras, watches and electrical goods. All this commerce makes the city's economy quite strong. Other industries are fishing, tourism and smuggling.

A resident of the enclaves can buy a car duty-free but must drive it in the enclave for one year before he can take it back to mainland Spain duty-free. In this way, you can buy a Mercedes, for example, at a price which is even below the price of the car in Germany.

ANDORRA

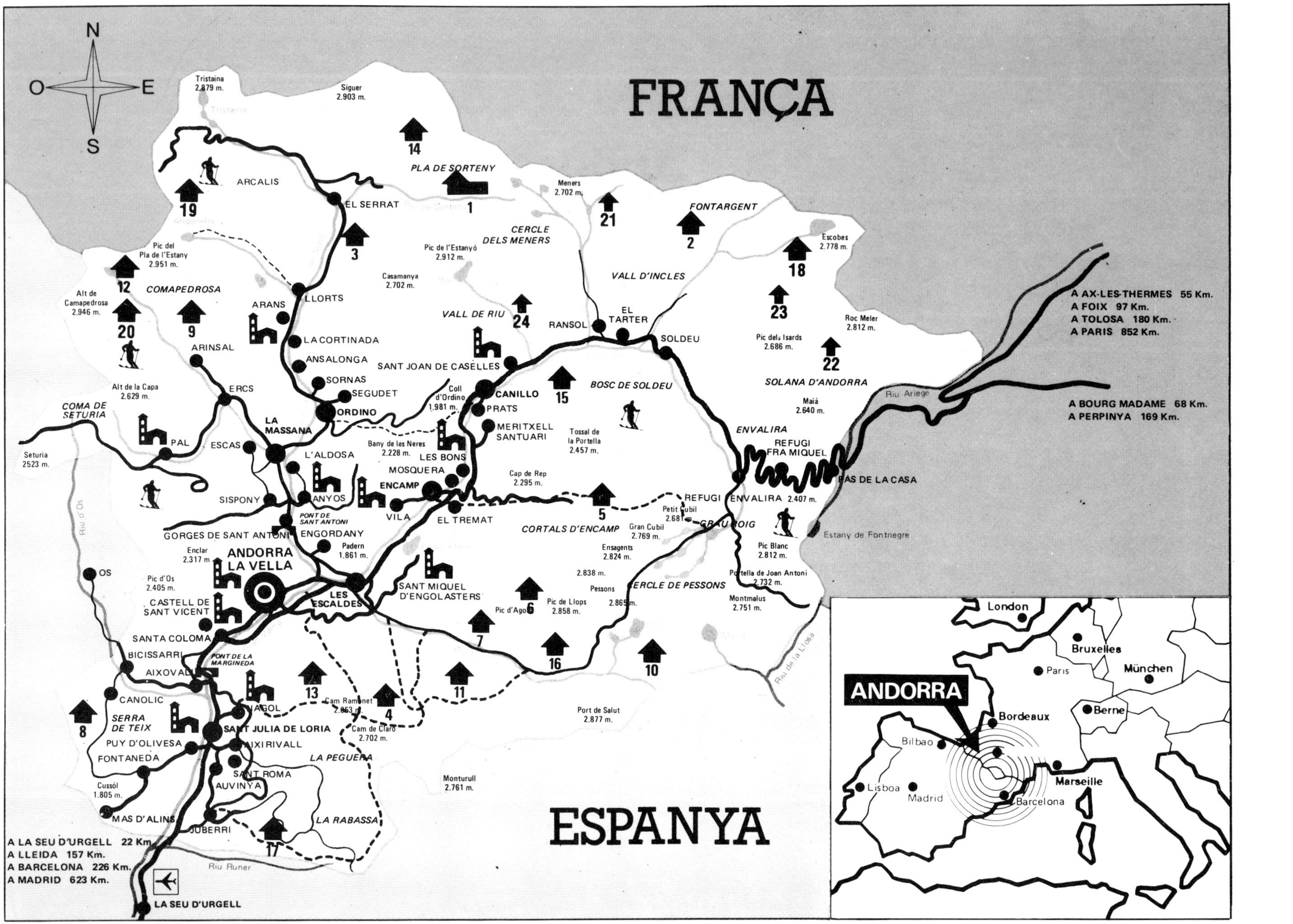

FRANÇA
ESPANYA
N
O
E
S
A AX-LES-THERMES 55 Km.
A FOIX 97 Km.
A TOLOSA 180 Km.
A PARIS 852 Km.
A BOURG MADAME 68 Km.
A PERPINYA 169 Km.
A LA SEU D'URGELL 22 Km.
A LLEIDA 157 Km.
A BARCELONA 226 Km.
A MADRID 623 Km.
LA SEU D'URGELL
Riu Runer
Riu Ariege
Riu d'Os
Riu de la Llosa
Tristaina 2.879 m.
Siguer 2.903 m.
PLA DE SORTENY
ARCALIS
EL SERRAT
Meners 2.702 m.
FONTARGENT
CERCLE DELS MENERS
Escobes 2.778 m.
Pic del Pla de l'Estany 2.951 m.
Pic de l'Estanyó 2.912 m.
COMAPEDROSA
Alt de Camapedrosa 2.946 m.
Casamanya 2.702 m.
VALL D'INCLES
VALL DE RIU
LLORTS
ARANS
LA CORTINADA
ANSALONGA
SORNAS
SEGUDET
ORDINO
ARINSAL
ERCS
RANSOL
EL TARTER
SOLDEU
Pic dels Isards 2.686 m.
Roc Meler 2.812 m.
SOLANA D'ANDORRA
SANT JOAN DE CASELLES
CANILLO
PRATS
MERITXELL SANTUARI
BOSC DE SOLDEU
Coll d'Ordino 1.981 m.
Maià 2.640 m.
Alt de la Capa 2.629 m.
COMA DE SETURIA
Seturia 2523 m.
PAL
ESCAS
LA MASSANA
L'ALDOSA
Bany de les Neres 2.228 m.
LES BONS
MOSQUERA
ENCAMP
Tossal de la Portella 2.457 m.
ENVALIRA
REFUGI FRA MIQUEL
PAS DE LA CASA
Cap de Rep 2.295 m.
REFUGI
ENVALIRA 2.407 m.
SISPONY
ANYOS
VILA
EL TREMAT
PONT DE SANT ANTONI
GORGES DE SANT ANTONI
ENGORDANY
Padern 1.861 m.
CORTALS D'ENCAMP
Petit Cubil 2.681
GRAU ROIG
Gran Cubil 2.769 m.
Estany de Fontnegre
Pic Blanc 2.812 m.
Enclar 2.317 m.
ANDORRA LA VELLA
Ensagents 2.824 m.
OS
Pic d'Os 2.405 m.
LES ESCALDES
SANT MIQUEL D'ENGOLASTERS
2.838 m.
Pessons
2.865 m.
CERCLE DE PESSONS
Portella de Joan Antoni 2.732 m.
Montmalus 2.751 m.
CASTELL DE SANT VICENT
Pic d'Agol
Pic de Llops 2.858 m.
SANTA COLOMA
BICISSARRI
AIXOVALL
PONT DE LA MARGINEDA
CANOLIC
SERRA DE TEIX
NAGOL
Cam Ramonet 2.853 m.
Cam de Claro 2.702 m.
Port de Salut 2.877 m.
SANT JULIA DE LORIA
PUY D'OLIVESA
AIXIRIVALL
FONTANEDA
LA PEGUERA
SANT ROMA
AUVINYA
Cussól 1.805 m.
MAS D'ALINS
JUBERRI
LA RABASSA
Monturull 2.761 m.
1
2
3
4
5
6
7
8
9
10
11
12
13
14
15
16
17
18
19
20
21
22
23
24
London
Bruxelles
Paris
München
Berne
ANDORRA
Bordeaux
Bilbao
Marseille
Lisboa
Madrid
Barcelona

ANDORRA IN A NUTSHELL: A PT'S OVERVIEW

Andorra is a pure tax haven. That means Andorra has never had any direct taxation of individuals and probably never will have an income tax in our lifetimes.

For someone who needs to get off tax rolls in his home country, by proving a new legal residence, it may be necessary to show unequivocally that you were accepted as a resident by a new and different country. Many governments do not feel it is legally possible for anyone to be a PT or perpetual tourist, without any fixed place of residence. There may be reasons that you cannot simply move yourself and your assets out of your present country of residence. If ass and assets can be moved, you do not need to be bothered with a tax haven residence! Moving your A & A may not be possible because you have substantial business interests or real estate that can't be liquidated. In such cases, it may be tax-advantageous to move to a lower-tax, or no-tax jurisdiction. In this case, Andorra is of definite interest. Andorra's Secret Nearby Enclaves could be of special interest to Germans or Scandinavians who are not permitted to move directly to a tax-haven but must make their move in two stages.

In Andorra, it is still possible to register and receive a government paper that you have applied for residence. The obtaining of the full permission is much more difficult than before, since the approval of the new law on immigration (October 1993). Forget about ever getting an Andorra passport though. Under present circumstances mere residence never gets you citizenship. Normally, the minimum requirement for residence is that you own a dwelling in Andorra. If you want to purchase or rent a large comfortable home or apartment and money is no object, then the selection is vast and the prices for a sumptuous home are considerably less than in any other tax haven. Likewise, there are ways to do it on the cheap with a purchase-leaseback or other deal involving a minimum level of accommodation. Servissim, an outfit in Andorra that helps new arrivals with their paperwork and home finding, offers counselling about the alternatives as part of their membership [see back pages for details].

The cheapest condo-apartments will probably cost around £40,000 for a "nothing special" studio. A very comfortable, large chalet with beautiful views would cost from £250,000 ($400,000) and up. (Note: Although we quote pounds sterling for the convenience of our British readers, prices in Andorra are normally quoted in Spanish pesetas, known locally as pessetas. However, property transactions can be made in any currency acceptable to both parties). The world-wide real estate depression hit Andorra slightly in 1993. Prices on average have dropped about 10 per cent from their all-time highs in 1991. But a well located, prime property is always saleable at a profit. The peseta was devalued in 1992 and again by 20 per cent in 1993. Thus bargains (in some foreign currency terms) are now available again.

As with stocks and bonds, whether past investments in Andorran homes are up or down is more dependent upon the currency of reference than the Andorran market. American investors in recent years would have trebled their money because the dollar, since 1985, has declined by almost two-thirds. Germans have lost money (in their terms) with the mark rising strongly against the peseta.

Currently, it is more difficult to sell most Andorra residential property (ie it takes longer) than in recent years and long term rental properties have become plentiful for the first time in memory as sellers decide to rent and wait.

We feel the most sensible thing is not to regard a home as an investment but to buy one only if you need one. As with spouses or art objects, it is better to acquire on a long term basis only those things you love or can't live without.

As all official business is conducted in the Catalan language, in any business dealings or government applications, some help will be needed from a bi-lingual English speaker. There are many real estate brokers and a large community of Brits already in Andorra.

Residence. A passport stamp showing the new residence, a lease or deed and/or an identity card is normally accepted as absolute proof of leaving the old country and having acquired a new fiscal address. For many countries, notably the USA and Great Britain, it is not usually necessary to prove residence by being accepted or having documentation from your new country or residence. These tax authorities will be satisfied if you merely do not live in their country any longer. This "non-residence" can be established by physically leaving and proving this with an exit stamp, and/or registering with the nearest Embassy or Consulate, which in both of the mentioned cases would be in Barcelona, Spain.

The USA (unique in the world for this) does not release citizens who move abroad from their obligation to file annual tax returns and pay taxes at the same rate as locals but it does give them $70,000 annual exemption on earned income. Americans can get a total exemption from all USA income taxes only by renouncing citizenship and acquiring a new passport. Brits and almost everyone else is relieved of tax burdens by merely moving abroad.

Sound reasons for acquiring a home or apartment in Andorra might include any of the following:

A) You like the country, and find the mountain climate invigorating.

B) You like to ski and prefer to have your own place on the slopes, not a rental.

C) You plan on running your international business or professional operations in a high-profile way and living in a tax haven allows you to escape most or all taxes.

A highly paid sports pro would be one type of person who'd have to prove he lived in another fiscal center to avoid a tax on income, capital gains or prize money earned in his former country of residence. Authors, film stars and anyone who does not need to live in a high-tax country to be able to produce a large income is a candidate for legal residence in a tax haven. Someone with substantial assets who invests or trades for a living is probably better off being an unregistered PT.

D) You want to bury black (untaxed) money in a real estate investment abroad where local rates (real estate municipal service charges) are very low giving you low holding costs.

E) You hope to make a profit on the resale of the property. Note: Although acquisition costs are not as heavy in Andorra as in most tax havens (around 2.5 per cent), the estate agent's fees are normally five per cent, so, to break even with a broker on each end of the deal, you will have to find a buyer who will pay 12.5 per cent more than you paid to enable you to break even. Speculating in real estate to make a short term profit is an unrealistic expectation in Andorra – especially in these times of deflation and devaluations. For those who buy well-constructed property in top locations taking the long view, returns should exceed inflation in the Spanish peseta.

F) **Last and most important**, you may find it psychologically impossible to be low profile. You want to make big deals, be on the cover of magazines, give lavish parties, drive an expensive car and live in an ostentatious house with Old Masters and designer furniture. At the same time, getting out of the tax net is so important to you that you are willing to permanently leave your old friends and family (or take them with you). In this case, you must live in a tax haven, and choosing between Bermuda, Monaco, Andorra and some of the others is just a matter of geographical and linguistic preference. Excuse the jargon. We just mean that you should choose your tax haven on the basis of strictly personal preference. Do you like the local ways of doing things? The climate? The general ambience? What you can afford is a consideration too. Presumably, anyone in this last category would not care if a top-of-the-line comfortable view home cost $500,000 as it might in Andorra or Campione, or upwards of $1,500,000 as it would in Bermuda or Monaco. But in all the other places you can rent! This makes initial entry costs in the more expensive tax havens cheaper and does not require a commitment of serious capital.

It was possible until 1991 to acquire an Andorran residence card by merely leasing a house or apartment without buying it. This is said to be difficult, if not impossible to pull off at the present time. An accommodation address is a possibility but normally such arrangements do not include or lead to obtaining a resident's card. If you wish to discuss the possibilities, please do so in a personal and confidential consultation with the Servissim people. But before you buy, remember, it may not be necessary to have a physical presence or legal residence in Andorra to accomplish your objectives. For many individuals, moving to a relatively high tax country like Italy, Spain or Great Britain can be just as effective and less costly than moving to a tax haven. It all depends upon your personal circumstances, goals and the particular rules and practices of your home country. It also depends on the passport(s) you hold or are willing to acquire. If the rules change, it is always easier to move A & A if you don't own property. This is the nutshell. For the big picture, read on.

THE HIDDEN COUNTRY

The mountaintop principality of Andorra as of 1992 unilaterally changed its ambiguous legal status for the first time in 700 years. A new constitution, unopposed by France and Spain, now makes it a "real country" with United Nations membership and the theoretical right to conduct its own foreign relations. Any real power or authority was withdrawn from its two princes (a

Spanish Bishop and the French Head of State) who now are mere figureheads (like the Queen of the United Kingdom in Canada) with only advisory powers. All effective political power is with the Council-General, elected by natural Andorrans – about 10,000 who were born there with two Andorran citizen parents. These voters represent only a small minority of the population. Disenfranchised (but not unhappy – for reasons to be discussed) are the approximately 30,000 Spanish, 15,000 Portuguese, 14,000 French and 15,000 other miscellaneous foreign residents.

Nothing really changed with the new constitution because its status as a self-governing nation was the reality in Andorra for over a decade and there has been a certain measure of self-government for the past century. But many relics of its old status as a "maybe-Spanish" and "maybe-French" province remain. There are still two competing postal systems (French and Spanish) and the telephone system, although run by the Andorran government, currently enjoys two international dialling codes, one via Spain and one via France. There are three school systems, French, Spanish and Andorran. A small tax on banks and corporations came into effect recently but individual income, estate and inheritance taxes still don't exist. Unfortunately, new taxes are not forbidden in the new constitution, either. But in our lifetimes personal income taxes in Andorra are as unlikely as an Africa free of corruption.

Geographically, Andorra is tucked away between France and Spain in the eastern Pyrenees. The closest major cities are Barcelona, Spain and Toulouse, France. The size of this country at 468 square-kilometers (just under 200 square miles) is much larger than places like Monaco, Liechtenstein or San Marino. Unbuildable mountain gradients take up about 90 per cent of the land area. By way of comparison, it is 50 times as big as Monaco which has about the same population. Obviously, there is far more elbow room, and less pollution in Andorra – at least once you get off the main street.

Andorra is a personal tax haven, a place to actually live or make your legal personal residence. For the time being it is not a good haven or base for "offshore" corporations who do not actually do business there.

Private individuals, however, will find Andorra a fine place to enjoy life or own a home in their own name. There are no income, capital gains, estate or inheritance taxes whatsoever. This is a contributing factor to the still-growing size of the very large expatriate population. These days many expatriates who used to live on the Spanish coast, plus quite a few

Spaniards themselves, have moved to Andorra to escape the ever more greedy Spanish tax-collectors. The Spanish IRS, by the way, is known as *the Hacienda.*

Tax is a bad word in Andorra. This translates to no direct taxes, no income taxes, no purchase taxes, no VAT, no profits taxes, no capital transfers taxes, no estate taxes, no death duties, no capital gains taxes. Are there any taxes at all? Yes. The government's major source of income is a small import tax mainly from cigarettes and motor fuel sold to shoppers from Spain and France. What Andorra doesn't have is what makes it a "near paradise". No pollution, no crime, no powerful government officials, no bureaucracy, very little red tape, no labor unions and politcal parties, only allowed since 1993, are still pretty ineffective.

Andorra has had uninterrupted political and economic stability for over 700 years.

Native Andorrans all have one other thing in their favor, **they know and recognize that nobody owes them a living**. No Andorran (aside from the tobacco farmers) gets any subsidy or free ride. These mountain people work hard, study hard and try to get ahead. Result – without any big fuss or fanfare they now have a privately owned, thriving local service economy. Their unregulated banking system is safe, sound, prosperous, computerised, streamlined, discreet and very customer-orientated.

The climate is crisp, alpine and pleasant. In the main town of Andorra la Vella (altitude approximately 900 meters), temperature is usually balmy and dry with cool nights in summer. Range 15 to 26 degrees Celsius. In the valley snow is rare even in winter. The winter temperature ranges from minus 7 to plus 8 Centigrade. This is 20 to 47 degrees Fahrenheit.

Rain and snow is plentiful. Like in mythical Camelot, much of the precipitation comes by night. The local tourist office claims 250 days of sunshine annually; this would leave about 110 cloudy and/or rainy days, a figure not far from reality. Humidity is low – and the climate seems beneficial to sufferers from arthritic or rheumatic conditions.

The SCENERY is outstanding, if you like mountains, that is. Go to Andorra for gorgeous peaks, valleys, lakes, streams, forests, quiet rustic villages and a bustling capital city. Endless shops stretch along the congested main road. Get off this road and you are in a different world. As far as day-to-day physical needs are concerned, the country is reasonably self-sufficient. Flooding gives them too much water at times! Hydro-electricity produces almost enough cheap electricity to serve local needs. But local demand has grown so fast that in recent years it has been necessary to purchase electricity from France and Spain. Water is the most important natural resource of the country. Besides power, there is a bottling industry which sells water such as *Font d'Arinsal* throughout northern Spain and southern France. Thermal springs around Les Escaldes provide heating for some houses and, because of the high sulphur content of the water, people with skin problems and rheumatism can benefit from bathing in it. A major water sports centre, costing £5 million, was due to open in December 1993 at the Centre Termoludic in Escaldes, under the name of Caldea.

In the past, Andorra industry included iron workings and some mineral mining, plus forestry. Much of the food supply is grown locally. Flocks of sheep, goats, horses and cattle graze contently on abundant vegetation.

Although Andorra currently has about 59,500 registered inhabitants, it has the lowest population density and largest land area of any tax haven we know of. Thus, the countryside is not crowded – once you get off the main shopping street. The main town and capital, Andorra la Vella, has a population of around 25,000. Of those registered in Andorra, about a quarter are Andorran. Sixty per cent are Spanish nationals (some 35,000). There are about 10,000 "other" foreigners. The second largest group are Portuguese, followed by French (4,000) and then Brits, about 1,000. A large number of Germans and Scandinavians add to the cosmopolitan atmosphere. A tiny American tax-exile enclave is to be found as well. Each group has some organised social activities. The official language of Andorra is called Catalan, a centuries-old romance language similar to Romanian and Swiss-Rumansch, spoken by about six million people around Barcelona. Spanish, called Castellano, is generally known. French is widely understood. You can get by with English too – but to a lesser extent.

NO CRIME – FREE HEALTH CARE

A recent world-wide actuarial survey featured in the *Economist* magazine detailed the average life-span of men and women. The longest-lived individuals live in Japan, and the shortest life-spans are reported from the Sudan; Andorrans came second to the Japanese by a reasonable margin. Crime is minimal there. Known law-violators promptly get the boot with swift deportations to their country of origin, usually Spain. The jail in Andorra is not really used much. Its six cells are locked only at night! There are strictly NO LABOR UNIONS. In fact, upper class Andorrans are so afraid of organised anything that they have effectively outlawed any form of legally organised political club, lodge or association. You will, however, find social security. In Andorra, this really DOES mean social security (not social insecurity as in most Western countries today where government is supposed to look after you).

Social Security in Andorra works. There is universal health and old age insurance for all employed persons. This includes hospital treatment, medical consultations and prescriptions, as well as indexed old age benefits. Non-employed residents may obtain medical coverage on a voluntary basis, the current cost of "CASS" being about 220,000 pesetas p.a. (about ££1,000 in 1993). Local medical and hospital facilities are good, comparing favorably with neighboring countries including those of Britain. Naturally, given the small size of the community, for treatment beyond a certain level of sophistication, hospitalisation outside Andorra may be required. Consequently, health care expenses incurred abroad are refunded by the Andorran social security system, subject to few restrictions.

Andorra offers two very good hospitals and has some 60 well qualified resident general practitioners and specialists on call. A third hospital was due to open before the end of 1993.

Dentists are equally competent, plentiful and very inexpensive. The government-run health insurance plan, provides medical care, dental coverage AND after at least 15 years of membership a small pension payable to all residents over 65!

Not bad for a place without any taxes! Employers and employees do however contribute to this social insurance scheme. More about this subject in a separate chapter.

Some sewage is believed to be pumped untreated into rivers and pollution is beginning to be seen to be a problem. La Massana has introduced fines up to 100,000 pesetas for throwing rubbish into rivers.

FREE MAIL, FREE SCHOOLS

There are many benefits to living in Andorra, apart from the absence of taxes. Andorra thrives so well off the small tax burden on her tourist industry and tobacco sales that many government services are FREE!

Mail service, for instance, is free within the country. Mail can be sent through either the French or Spanish postal systems. Take your pick. Both postal systems supply their own picturesque Andorran stamps. The French is faster but more expensive.

Another valuable freebie? French and Spanish schools accept students free of charge, books included. In future years there may be a premium to be paid by permanent foreign residents who wish to have their children educated there. At present, the only cost of education to the "baccalaureat" level is transport. For about $150 a year, your children can be driven door-to-door between school and home in new Mercedes mini-buses. For a Catalan education, Andorra has a third school system supported by the local government.

Like Andorran mail, two different phone systems are available. French, dialling code from London is 010-33-628, for Spanish Andorra, dial 010-34-734. Line quality is not the best on the Spanish system, though not any worse than in the rest of the Iberian peninsula. The French service is more technically advanced. Direct dial telephones, telex, fax are all available. They usually work. International calls are cheaper from booths than hotels.

Direct taxes are NOT going to be introduced in the foreseeable future. The electorate has shown DEEP aversion to the introduction of any form of direct taxation, ie income or wealth taxes.

The main indirect "customer tax" is the import duty. This adds a few percentage points to the price of cigarettes, petrol, alcohol, cars and perfume. This duty generates some 99 per cent of budget revenues. Because the majority of goods sold locally are actually consumed in France or Spain, the burden of these taxes falls on the tourists. This explains the high tax returns from low rates. No Value Added Tax or VAT equivalent exists.

RESTAURANTS FOR GOURMET DINING – DELI TREATS

In Andorra, there is a wide range of restaurants and hotels. Some new hotels are like five-star luxury establishments. No restaurants in Andorra have earned any Michelin star-class ratings. We reckon this to be the case mainly because Andorra is off the beaten track of the Michelin reviewers. We would give a star or two to several restaurants and hotels described elsewhere in this report.

Food markets and shops carry an outstanding variety of products at the lowest prices in Europe. Any imported delicatessen treat or sweet thing conceivable can be purchased locally.

CHEAP OR FREE ENTERTAINMENT

There are four movie houses, a myriad of clubs and discos, and an annual procession of regional festivals. Take your choice, folk dancing, street dancing, auto and motorcycle racing. Almost all are free. You can rent video films in English.

A local radio station, Radio Valira, broadcasts on frequencies 93.3 FM and 98.1 FM. It keeps residents and visitors informed on current and forthcoming events. The English language program goes on the air from 2.30 to 3 pm every day from Monday to Friday. Tune in once you get there and listen to lively Karen Hadden. Or if you need any information about where to meet people of similar inclinations when in the country, contact the International Club of Andorra. Tony Hooper, telephone 36152, can give details.

HOTELS IN ANDORRA

In our first *Andorra Report* published in 1991, we regretted that there were no world class or even first class hotels in the country. The best listings in the official tourist guides were those independent or international franchise operators like Best Western or Novotel catering to the package tour crowd. The last Andorra Report echoed the official line that local accommodation and food were certainly interesting, substantial and good value for money – but not for the discriminating or sophisticated palate.

Then we received a letter from an Andorra resident taking exception to our remarks that there wasn't a single five star hotel or first class restaurant in the whole country. Our correspondent, Simon Binsted, a Brit who moved to Andorra from South Africa ten years ago, runs a business (Servissim) helping new residents acquire property, comply with local paperwork and generally find their way about. His letter said: "Visit us again, and my wife Maria Teresa and I will personally escort you to a few restaurants and hotels that you will find world-class and praiseworthy." Simon Binsted and his Catalonian wife were true to their word.

During our last visit he took us to a few of his favorite places, as I will duly report upon here. In return, we promised to give his well established Andorra company, Servissim, and his monthly English-language newsletter on Andorra a good plug. For his address and fee schedule, see Resource Section at end of text. These are a few of his favorites and our recent discoveries:

ANDORRA PARK HOTEL & RESTAURANT, Carrer les Canals, Andorra La Vella, phone: 20979, fax: 28329. It has the most convenient location for a day of shopping and doing business. It's Very Downtown just behind the Pyrenees department store (biggest emporium in Andorra). If a hotel guest, you can park on the exquisite park-like hotel grounds and then visit the most congested shopping and commercial areas by simply walking a few meters over to the top floor of the Pyrenees parking garage (same level as the hotel). Take their elevator six floors down to a different world – the level of main street, known as Avinguda Meritxell.

The very existence of this rather sizeable establishment seems to be one of the many well-kept secrets of Andorra. It seemed to me that you can find out about "The Park", only through a local. On prior visits to Andorra, I saw no signs or billboards for this grand old hotel. It is pre-War but was completely restored in 1988. Neither was it listed in any tourist guide. I asked our new friend Simon why this hotel was so low profile. I am not sure if he was pulling my leg but his answer was that the owner, a local chap, is so rich, that he prefers his hotel and restaurant to be run as what amounts to a private club for those in the know. The requirement for "membership" accordingly, is that you **know** about the place and can **find your way there**. Both are hard to do without local help. Unless you are a reader of this book, of course.

For your first visit to the Park Hotel, you can always park in the Pyrenees garage, an easy thing to find, as The Pyrenees department store is the major landmark of Andorra. Parking in the Pyrenees garage is free for two hours to any shopper who spends 3000 pesetas (around £10), otherwise there's an hourly rate. Go to the top floor of the garage with your car or by elevator and there you'll see a small sign for the Park Hotel. The hotel directly adjoins the parking building. But this is not nearly as bad as it sounds because the hotel is on beautifully landscaped grounds a bit above the top floor of the garage. You'll be as amazed as I was to exit an ordinary big city garage, via its roof, to see a sedate old-world hotel set in a remarkably beautiful and tranquil lawn and rock-garden. The hotel is above the hustle, bustle, traffic and congestion of half-a-million busy shoppers trundling about 70 feet below.

Once you get to the hotel, or by telephone, the hotel staff will direct you how to get your car into their own parking area – available at no charge if you are going to spend a night or two. If you fiddle around enough and ask questions, you will eventually negotiate the one-way streets and find it on your own. Expensive by local standards, you will be a pampered guest at this hotel and dine for about 30 per cent of London prices for equivalent accommodations. It has "A" class rooms with view, and "B" class rooms, similar in size, but with no view. Class "B" costs about a third less. We popped for the top-of-the-line and had a gorgeous balcony plus view room for 21,000 pesetas, with half-board. We also had a bath-tub built for two but I don't know if this is in all rooms or we were just lucky. At the exchange rate then existing, it was about £100 or $150 per night. This includes use of an amazing pool fed by warm air running down a rock-face as if from a mountain stream. There is also tennis, mini-golf, croquet, and a first class à la carte meal in the deluxe restaurant would be around 5,000 pesetas. Let the waiter (in a tux, naturally) recommend a selection of house specialities. You won't be disappointed. Specialities are printed in red on the multi-lingual menu. You can take a room with board or without board. As you'd probably eat breakfast and either lunch or dinner in the hotel anyway, it is a good idea to take half-board. Full board (breakfast and two meals) offers rather more than most of us can eat.

Another discovery hotel, slightly less costly, is the new **Xalet Ritz at Sispony**, just outside of, and on a mountainside overlooking, La Massana. This place is easy to find, and has a gourmet restaurant almost as good as the Park. Try to get a view room facing La Massana if you want to see a sparkling fairyland from your bed at night. The same suggestion about signing on for half-board applies here but there is no chance of your getting bored with the same menu. Why? The hotel has arranged for you to take at your choice of two nearby establishments (same ownership – different chefs), both of them very good: Borda de l'Avi or Xopluc. The Xalet Ritz has a swimming pool and there is tennis tennis and heated parking (good for the winter).

The above hotels are both five-star and when we visited, there wasn't a tour bus in sight.

The only five-star hotel in Andorra is the Roc Escaldes. As it has not been open long, we have not been able to sample it personally but would welcome any readers' views.

For additional hotels said to be good value for money, see the resource list at end of this book.

OTHER HOTELS OF INTEREST (JUST OUTSIDE ANDORRA)

SPAIN

If you arrive (or leave) in a car via Seo d'Urgel, Spain, you'll be glad I suggested you spend the night at the famous three star parador (government owned hotel and restaurant) inside a Fourteenth Century Dominican convent. It has an indoor pool and pretty good restaurant. As with all paradors, the prices are reasonable, for what you get, and the architecture here is very unusual for a hotel. The paradors of Spain and Portugal are often built inside lovingly restored national monuments that a private developer couldn't ever touch for love nor money. Because the roads into and out of Andorra can be very jammed up from about 8 am to 8 pm, it is not a bad idea to leave this parador early in the morning and have a traffic free ride into Andorra. Then you can get settled in your Andorra hotel or apartment before the one main road gets too hectic. At Seo you are only about 20 minutes to Andorra. Phone: (Spain) 973-35-20-00 or fax: 35-23-09.

Also in La Seo there is, some say, an even better choice and that is the Hotel Castell, 1km out on the road to Lleida. Set in the old castle walls with spectacular views over the whole valley and the town of La Seo, the food is reputed to be the best in the area.

Further away, in the direction of Barcelona, there's another parador, even more interesting from an architectural point of view, and a bit more classy (four star). The Parador de Cardona, phone: (93) 869-1275 or fax: 869-1636, is a primitive, but magnificent structure – a castle-fortress started by Charlemagne around 800 AD and finished over a thousand years ago! the interior modernization is first class. This one is about an hour from the Andorra border. There are about 90 paradors in Spain (similar ones in Portugal) and you can make your reservations via any Spanish Government Tourist Office. There's one in Andorra at Carlemany 105, Escaldes. Phone: 29-303.

FRANCE

The Germans have an expression for "good living", and it is *Wie Gott in Frankreich.* What it means is that Germans feel if God ever came down to live the good life on Earth he'd settle in

France. In terms of food and hotels, the Germans are right. It is hard to find better quality, especially in restaurants, than in France. Even in a small, remote country inn, the standards are amazingly high, and just an ordinary meal at an ordinary place is the equivalent of a very expensive French restaurant anywhere else in the world. When driving cross-country, I like to stay at a place known for its food. That way I can enjoy a leisurely two or three hour dinner, with wine and retire to my room without having to drive somewhere else.

If you want a real treat coming into Andorra from France, there are a number of possibilities. You can hardly go wrong stopping anywhere bearing the green sign of the Logis de France organization of independent hoteliers. A step up and you'll look for the logo of the *Chaine des Rotisseurs*, Romantik Hotels, or *Relais du Silence*. These are all organizations whose members (throughout the world but mainly in France) adhere to certain high standards.

In the village of Llo, not far from Bourg Madame, try the L'Atalaya for a Spanish/French menu. The price of a double room is about £50 and a first class dinner with wine, about £20. Phone: France (33) 6804-7004 or fax: 6804-0129.

CASE HISTORY #1: TWO AMERICANS

According to our favorite travel newsletter *International Living,* Americans Richard le Grelle (real name) and wife fled the fast lane of the Hollywood Hills to escape the smog, crime and skyrocketing cost of living.

Now they live in Ordino, Andorra, close to stores, banks, pharmacies, a butcher who raises his own cattle, a general store stocking American and British newspapers, French and Spanish post offices and schools. Their neighbors in Ordino are a mixture of English, French and Spanish speaking retired professionals. Vacation home owners include wealthy European and several Australians. Because of the low crime rate, Mr le Grelle never locks his door or his cars. "Local people", he states, "are extremely amicable. We've met and made friends with more people here in one month than we had for three years in California. We never run out of things to do, either. Dinner and cocktail parties occur frequently."

As Richard le Grelle continues: "My wife and I are now adopted Andorrans. We have a beautiful home, a nice car. We enjoy all the comforts we had in California without any of the drawbacks. And at half the cost".

CASE HISTORY #2: TWO CANADIANS

One of our readers, Mr Garvin (not his real name), made the move from Canada to Gibraltar, then from Gibraltar to Andorra. In a letter to us he writes:

"Andorra has an easy, open residence policy provided you are of moderately independent means and not a crook or gangster. If they find out you are, they'd peremptorily sling you out. Ditto if you got your nose dirty here. Police authorities here are strong and quite arbitrary. But they are dedicated to keeping trouble out. It is absolutely physically beautiful as few places are. Once you get off the heavily-travelled main highway and up into the side roads in the mountains, it is lovely, peaceful, quiet, filled with wild flowers, birds and wildlife, pure mountain streams everywhere – balm to the soul. Now if what you want is to watch the jet-set posing and posturing; and if you are not happy unless you can blow a few thousand bucks every night at the casino, then I guess Monaco is your kind of town! But the fact that Andorra is not Monaco and is not on the Cote d'Azur or the Costa del Sol doesn't, in my book, make it beneath consideration as a place to live. Besides, it's a real tax haven. The people are strongly libertarian. In fact, they invented the philosophy of anarchism. Scratch a Libertarian and you get an anarchist just beneath the surface. Contrary to popular belief, this anarchistic way of thinking just means that **local people look after local interests** – without Big Brother central bureaucracies. Privacy is respected!"

Mr Garvin, like Mr le Grelle, found himself a nice chalet in Andorra. He now lives with a girlfriend in this high altitude home not far from Ordino.

CLASSICAL MUSIC, CONCERTS & JAZZ FESTIVALS

Ordino, or rather the National Auditorium in Ordino, plays host to the annual Festival Internacional de Musica, now in its eleventh year. The program consists of six concerts of classical music performed by internationally renowned musicians. Andorra may not have the high cultural level of say, Israel, but it is second only to Monaco in the tax-haven league for quality music, ballet, and visiting theatre troupes.

In the huge sports pavilion in Escaldes/Engordany, the annual International Jazz Festival of Andorra is staged every year in August. Regulars are such names as Miles Davis, Teto

Montoliu, Ray Barreto, Larry Carlton and the Stanley Clark/Georges Duke Project. The expatriate community supports a lively cultural life.

IS ANDORRA YOUR CUP OF TEA?

The reader mentioned above, Mr Garvin, wrote to us to tell the tale of his recent move from Gibraltar to Andorra. While researching Andorra on his own, he hopped over to Monaco for a couple of weeks to check out the place, having purchased the *Monaco Report* available from Scope International. [See order form in the back of this report.] Here's his verdict:

"Your reports proved mind-bending for me and my lady. Much food for thought. Monaco was quite a circus, not the place for us I'm afraid. We are as weird and unconventional as you are but just not into glitter, big money and gawking at jetset personalities. Have now concluded from own adhoc enquiries that Andorra is best place for us. Snows in winter. After 12 years away from Canada, we miss the stuff. There are very few formalities, very little bureaucracy and no difficulties about living here. We enjoy an exceptionally good life-style at very low cost. It's a relaxed, crime-free atmosphere with lovely weather. What more can I say? Do come and visit us. See for yourself."

So we did. We discovered that Andorra probably is the place in Europe with the highest number of Mercedes, BMWs and Range Rovers per capita. It is also home base to around 80,000 PTs!

CHOOSING THE BEST OF ANDORRA'S 250 RESTAURANTS

Dining out in Andorra? This involves a choice between more than 250 different restaurants! Due to a population consisting two-thirds of foreigners, there is a great variety in cuisine.

Meals are leisurely affairs, with lunches often taking up most of the afternoon. Or half the night for dinner! Prices are reasonable and on a par with northern Spain. As in Spain, an "early" dinner starts at 9.30 pm and often ends after midnight.

Where to dine? We suggest the Moli del Peano at Canillo. You are close to the French border and will discover that it is indeed possible to get first class French cuisine in Andorra.

This recommended establishment, directed by members of the Hetch-Fouquat family, is inside an old mill whose interior mimics the grandly bourgeois hostelries of its giant neighbor to the north. The restaurant, open daily except Monday, offers three different menus at around 1250 pesetas, 1750 pesetas and 2500 pesetas. A la Carte meals will cost around 1800 pesetas. Recommended: The outdoor terrace on a sunny day.

In Anyos, the restaurant Can Pere, recently taken over by cosmopolitan Oscar von der Lanken, is very popular with the English-speaking community, with excellent international dishes at reasonable prices.

Another favorite. When in Les Escaldes, try El Pi, at 5 Placa dels Co-Princeps, tel: 21486, for the best recipes of France and Spain and wines from both countries as well. Has its own spa too!

Our own top of the el cheapo list is the Restaurant Hotel Europa, 57 Avinguda Carlemany, still in Les Escaldes. Fixed-priced meals at an ultra-low $5 a meal consist of three courses, soup, a main course with vegetables, and a dessert. Nice spacious atmosphere and effective, polite service.

Other good spots: Borda de l'Avi in La Massana where they cater to many English residents. The Borda Calissa or the Restaurant La Neu, close by each other, are good when you visit the lively ski-resort of Arinsal. Try Borda d'Arans in Arans. You'll also like the Xalet at Erts. Borda does not mean restaurant, by the way. It is the local word for "barn."

The best restaurant in the whole country is in the Park Hotel in Andorra La Vella.

In Andorra, free outdoor concerts usually begin at 10 pm, allowing a decent interval between the outdoor activities of the day and the relaxing entertainment of the night. And you can still get a dinner or a nightcap when the band stops playing. Most bars close late and some are open the maximum allowed. That means they close only from 4 am to 6 am.

In Andorra, much more than elsewhere, the owner of a business gets to regulate business hours, non-smoking sections, wages and hours, prices and what is stocked. The market not Big Brother decides if he will succeed.

SHOPPING IN EUROPE'S BARGAIN BASEMENT

The majority of shops and supermarkets keep Spanish hours. They are open every day until about 8 o'clock in the evening, except for Sundays, when "early closing" is more like 7 to 7.30

pm. September 8 (national holiday), Christmas, New Year's Day and Good Friday are the only days when all stores are closed.

Andorra is the shopper's dream. Prices are lower for almost everything than anywhere else in Europe. Appealing bargains can be found on items from Japanese electronics to high fashion apparel. What's more, residents can get local **credit cards for discounts**. These discounts, usually around 10 per cent, are then deducted from your bill each month!

Cash, pesetas or francs, is preferred in most shops and a few will take credit cards or checks but many traders are unwilling to accept these or make a surcharge if they do. Andorran prices can be amazingly low. Where else can you get a bottle of Chivas Regal for US $8? If one compares Andorran prices with French prices, the differential is more than the VAT saving, which alone is 18 per cent to 30 per cent. Booze and cigarettes are much cheaper than in France or Spain. Shops in Andorra la Vella include Christian Dior, Cellini, Cacharel – the whole Rodeo Drive set. Pyrenees is the largest department store. It is affiliated with the renowned Printemps of Paris. Although it looks up-market from the outside it carries only the LATEST in everything and at bargain prices. In Pyrenees, the second-floor food market rivals Harrod's of London. The liquor department, facing stiff price competition from the hypermercados, sells only the best brands at discount prices.

If shopping is your game, set aside a week to explore the boutiques in Andorra la Vella, the capital. It is a modern city, dominated by Charlemagne (Carlemany) Avenue, the two-and-a-half mile main street named after one of the founding fathers, and Avenue Meritxell (pronounced Merry-chay). The streets are rimmed with shops, banks, theaters, cafes and restaurants. The townspeople are well-dressed. New cars are everywhere and the city exudes prosperity.

SHOPPING TIPS

The main road running through Andorra is perhaps the world's longest shopping mall. The quantity and variety of good on offer is staggering. The only other place in the world that can exceed it being Singapore. Prices in Andorra are generally lower than in Singapore with a few exceptions we note here.

WHAT'S WORTH A SPECIAL TRIP?

Booze, tobacco, auto-parts and auto-supplies. These items are probably as cheap as anywhere in the world. Gasoline and diesel are so cheap that you can afford to acquire a trunk full of filled jerricans for about the same price as the gas alone across the border. If you arrive in winter, by all means get a set of snow chains. They are not cheap, they are required by law to be carried in your car and used when snow is on the road.

GO OUT OF YOUR WAY FOR IT IF YOU'RE THERE ALREADY

Perfumes, candy, running shoes, ski-equipment (Note: Package deals often offer skis, boots, poles and clothes at the price of skis and boots alone), name-brand fashion items, jewelry, watches, cameras, electronics are all slightly cheaper than at most airport duty-free stores and half the retail prices of Paris, Madrid or London. There are also always special sales and reduced merchandise that offer the well-informed shopper the occasional super-deal. In general, prices on popular items are at least one-third below similar items in France or Spain. Food, especially cheese, hams, and exotic delicatessen is also available with a selection hard to duplicate outside of Harrod's Food Halls in London. Super or hyper markets include Jumbo, Mamut and Sant Eloi – all with free parking for customers. Department stores (also offering free parking with any purchase) are Punt de Trobada, just inside the Spanish border, and slightly down market from the more famous Pyrenees Department store in Andorra La Vella. Both are highly recommended.

Cars are bargains compared to most places, but do some comparison shopping before you come. A Fiat Cinquecento or Panda will probably be cheaper (tourist delivery price) in Spain. A Ford, BMW, Volkswagen or Mercedes may be cheaper in Denmark, Belgium, Holland or Switzerland. The best deals in Andorra are probably on Japanese, Russian or USA made four-wheel drive vehicles and motorcycles. You will get one-year tourist plates when you purchase the cars. They are not tax free but the tax is only seven per cent.

WHAT NOT TO BUY!

Computers, software and related equipment are on display but these are not generally good deals for English-speaking buyers. The reason is that such equipment on sale in Andorra is targeted for Spanish or French speakers. Instruction books and screen messages may thus be incomprehensible for our readers. The best bargains are found in the American mail-order catalogs and, with the cheap air-fares to the USA, it is almost worth a trip for items priced at three or four times as much in Europe or double in London. Because of volume and competitiveness, London is the second best place to buy computers. In Hong Kong and Singapore, hardware prices are about the same as in America but dealers are well know for "throwing in" software that is worth perhaps three times the value of the computers.

ANDORRA RATED AS A SEX HAVEN

Although the financial base for the – very small, but large enough for Andorra – government budget is largely "booze and tobacco, perfume and petrol", Andorra is really not the place to go for abundant sexual opportunities.

It is a wonderful place to retire, let there be no doubt about that. And the tiny country is very cosmopolitan due to the overwhelming numbers of foreigners living there. But dating and mating there (with the locals anyway) is solely a game for the serious. With the Catholic church still in a strong position, you must talk of marriage to score with the old fashioned local girls.

A leading political figure in government, Mr Jaume Bartumeu, has vowed to change some of archaic laws still imposed on Andorra by the Spanish church. There is no divorce. The death penalty for many crimes existed right up until 1992 but had not been imposed since 1954. The last public execution by firing squad took place opposite the Town Hall in Andorra la Vella in 1943 and pictures of the event can be seen at the police station and many other places including on the waiting room wall of one of the Notaries. Sexy magazines, including the relatively tame *Playboy*, are still banned from news stands. Prostitution is illegal and not tolerated. As a result, no "hostess joints" or sex shows of any kind are to be found in Andorra. Rumor has it, however, that a couple of "escorts" are working low profile out of the British expat-ghetto of La

Massana. As a rule of thumb, Andorra is most certainly no sex haven. But tourists come in droves to ski, to dance, to smell the flowers and to make new friends. As in any resort playground, the girls are looking for romance. Boys look for girls who are looking for romance. Presto, romance! But not much instant gratification.

The Andorrans have found a subtle revenge against the puritanism of one of their rulers, the Bishop of Seu d'Urgell. They are opening several brothels in the Spanish section of his diocese. Although the bishop can stop such naughtiness in Andorra, he cannot do so in Spain, which has softer laws on girls earning a living in the laid-back manner.

For middle-aged men in very good shape there is an abundance of "snow bunnies" or young British girls who come to Andorra during the winter to ski. They work at the many aprés-ski night clubs with live (modern) music. Despite heavy competition from good looking young studs, the Andorran ski slopes or the crowded aprés-ski bars and restaurants could be your happy hunting ground. But don't look for the professional courtesans of Bangkok in Ordino or St Julia. Thailand it isn't. The local girls will exchange sweet talk, wining and dining, walks in the moonlight. Then, with a little bit of luck you might get a kiss or two. Your next destination will be the altar, not the bedroom.

ANDORRA: GETTING THERE – OPTIONS

The bad news, Andorra is way off the beaten track. The good news, you'll get there. Eventually.

Distances are (in kilometres): From Barcelona 200, from Madrid 620, from Paris 880 and from Toulouse 180. Flying gets you close but not on the spot. There is no airport, nor even a private airstrip within Andorra. In terms of time, there is now not much to choose between Toulouse and Barcelona but, in terms of international services, Barcelona is much better. Although on the map Gerona, in Spain, would appear closer, the travelling time through the mountains is much greater and these days Gerona airport used only by some charter flights.

In both cases after air arrival, about three hours of additional winding mountain road travel must be contemplated. Your best bet is to hire a car, take a public bus from the airports or, if you're in Barcelona, grab a rental car or one of the very reasonably priced taxicabs. The price for a taxi to Andorra will be about US $100. Make sure, however, to always agree on taxi prices in advance. If you don't, you will pay double the meter price since the driver insists he must go back empty and you've got to cover it. A cheaper share-taxi service at 4000 pesetas a seat, which must be booked, runs both from central Barcelona and the airport twice daily.

The essential point to remember is that Andorra is literally a hidden valley nestled in the Pyrenees mountain range with one road – and only one – leading to France. There is also one road – and only one – leading to Spain. Going between France and Spain via Andorra is definitely the long way round. But millions of people do it each year for the scenery and the bargain shopping.

The only nearby general aviation field, limited to small planes, is near Martinet, a Spanish village some 50 miles (80 km) away. This town has no customs and immigration facilities but these days, for air taxi or personal flights within the EC, it is generally not necessary to worry about customs any more. The (Spanish) army-run domestic airport at La Seu d'Urgell (about 20 km from Andorra-center) is no longer available for civilian traffic. With that deactivation, Andorran dreams of their own commercial airport next door have been put to rest for the time being. Building a small airport and establishing an air-taxi service would probably be a good business for someone with an Andorran partner.

If you come by rail, coming from the north (Paris/Switzerland), the closest station available is on the French side, at L'Hospitalet.

OUR SECRET: THE BEST WAY TO GET TO ANDORRA

Consider the special night train, complete with dining and sleeping cars, coming from Paris. This stops at the small village of L'Hospitalet (five miles from the Franco-Andorran border) every morning at around 7.30 am. A connecting bus drops you off in Andorra "Centro" about an hour later.

Note that over-65's can travel for half-fare on French trains with a "carte vermeil". For those who can't afford $500 per day on the Orient Express, the Paris-Andorra train is a bargain substitute at 950 francs (£95) coach sleeping car, one way. You can use the Inter-rail pass for this trip, of course. For any tourist who will be doing a lot of travelling in any given month, the Eurail travel pass can reduce your costs by up to 90 per cent.

SHOULD YOU OWN A CAR?

As in California, having a car is almost a "must" when living in Andorra. The feeder motorways (toll) are the Barcelona-Madrid axis on the Spanish side and the Atlantic-Mediterranean motorway from Bordeaux to Narbonne on the other side. Use any of these exits for Andorra: Toulouse, Carcassone or Perpignan.

The actual driving time from Switzerland is at least eight hours, from Paris at least ten. Not to be overlooked in the winter, from the French side, the mountain pass road to Andorra climbs to a snowbound 2409 meters. Snow clearance on this road is reasonably prompt and effective. Very seldom does one have to wait more than a few hours at maximum for roads closed by snow or avalanche to be re-opened for traffic.

The roads into Andorra recently have improved greatly but some sections still are narrow, winding and dangerous. Fast freeways are under construction on the Spanish side. The old-fashioned two lane highways, often clogged with smoke-belching diesel trucks, are rapidly being replaced by freeways. Incidentally, when you get into France, don't make the same mistake I did. Pulling into a self service gas station and confronted with pumps labelled "Essence" and "Gasoil" I went for the "Gasoil". It wasn't gasoline, but diesel. My new car didn't run and I lost a day after being towed to a repair shop where they flushed out the tank and engine.

MOTOR VEHICLES – OVERVIEW

As a foreigner visiting Andorra you, and anyone else who does not have Andorran residency, are not allowed to own or purchase any type of motor vehicle which is registered on Andorran plates, and neither may you apply for an Andorran driving licence. However, there are no regulations to prevent you from insuring or driving any vehicle in Andorra which you own or which you have permission to use, and which is registered in another country.

As usual in Andorra, those are the rules, and, also as usual, there are ways around them...

DRIVING IN ANDORRA

First the good news. If you're one of those drivers who's never in the right gear at the right time, or you tend to wander across to the other side of the road on bends, or jump traffic lights and ignore speed limits, pedestrian crossings, stop signs and so on, just relax. Nobody's even going to notice because all the Andorrans drive just like you!

Now the bad news. If you're not a driver like that, you're going to find driving in Andorra a bit unnerving. The best plan is to drive down through France because the French are nearly as bad and that will at least give you time to get used to it.

The specific problem with Andorran drivers seems to be compulsion. If an Andorran sees a car on the road in front of him (or her – the women are just as bad), he is compelled to overtake it, or die in the attempt.

It doesn't matter if he is driving a Renault 5 and the car in front is a Porsche 911 Turbo or if he is only a hundred yards or so from his destination or turning. He **has** to overtake, and you will, when driving in Andorra, frequently experience the sensation of having a car surge past you, usually at or approaching a blind corner and then have to do an emergency stop as that same car brakes hard to turn off the road into a hotel car park.

What is particularly striking is how markedly this behaviour on the road contrasts with the usual Andorran pace of life, which is lethargic at best. Only behind the wheel of a vehicle, it seems, does any Andorran move at any speed.

A revised highway code for Andorran drivers was introduced with effect from 21 January 1992. Some of the more important regulations are:

1. Crash helmets must be worn by all motorcyclists;
2. Drivers must give way to the right, just as in France, unless there are road markings or signs to the contrary;
3. Drivers must carry driving licenses and insurance certificates at all times; drivers who cannot produce this documentation can be fined and/or immobilised on the spot;
4. The maximum blood-alcohol level is now 80mg, and drivers can insist on a blood test;

5. Sensible new no-parking regulations now apply. You may not stop on blind corners, pedestrian crossings, bridges, intersections, in tunnels or where you would force other drivers to cross a solid white line, and neither may you park with your car facing the "wrong" direction. "Abusive" or obstructive stopping or parking in urban areas is forbidden. Yellow lines at the side of the road indicate whether parking is permitted – a yellow zigzag or solid yellow line means no stopping or parking; if there is a broken yellow line, you have to check the restriction plate to see what the parking regulations are.

LICENSES

The usual licensing rules apply, in that you are allowed to drive any vehicle in Andorra which you are licensed to drive in your home country, and your normal national license is perfectly acceptable as proof of your driving competence. This applies to residents of all countries which were signatories to the International Convention of 1949. The most glaring omission to this convention was the United States. US licenses are issued by the individual states and, therefore, not always recognized internationally so although there is unlikely to be any problem for tourists, exchanging these for an Andorran license once resident can present certain problems.

INTERNATIONAL LICENSES

An international driving license is not generally required, though some Spanish policemen, especially those "out in the sticks", still like to see one.

ANDORRAN DRIVING LICENSES

If you are granted a residence permit, you are obliged to apply for an Andorran driving license, in exchange for your original license, within six months of receiving your residency document. As the Andorran authorities insist on retaining your original driving license, it is a good idea to apply for a replacement license, saying that the original has been lost or stolen, to your national licensing authority. A man can't have too many driving licenses, or too many passports...

There is not usually any requirement to take a driving test prior to the issue of an Andorran license but a short medical examination will need to be arranged.

DOCUMENTS TO BE CARRIED

On a related topic, remember that if you are driving in France or Spain in your own car, you are required to carry the vehicle's registration document or equivalent with you. If the vehicle is not your own, then you need a photocopy of the registration document, plus written and signed permission from the vehicle's owner allowing you to use it.

COMPULSORY ITEMS

Please remember that the carriage of spare bulbs for the vehicle, with a warning triangle for use in breakdowns, are compulsory throughout Europe. Some countries also insist on the carriage of other items, such as a first-aid kit, as well. In some countries, including Andorra, if a policeman is feeling really grim and you wear spectacles for driving, he can also fine you for not having a spare pair.

In the winter, a set of **correct size** snow chains is also a compulsory item in Andorra and between L'Hospitalet and Pas de la Casa in France.

INSURING A 'FOREIGN' CAR

Vehicle insurance in Andorra is expensive, partly because the Andorrans are arguably the worst drivers in Europe and partly because there is no such thing as a previous no-claims bonus in the eyes of Andorra-based insurance companies. And there are problems, especially for United Kingdom residents, if attempts are made to insure a vehicle for permanent use in Andorra through a non Andorra-based company.

The general rule is that a vehicle must be insured in the country in which it will be most frequently used and in which it will be garaged or parked when not in use. So, for a three-week trip to Andorra, there is no problem – your insurance company will simply issue you with a

Green Card and extend your normal insurance cover to the wilds of Europe. But if you live abroad, that's another matter entirely.

ANNUAL GREEN CARD

There is, with changes in EC border regulations and the imminent opening of the Channel Tunnel, an increasing perception among some British insurance companies that Britain might just perhaps be considered to be a part of Europe. This perception has been translated by some companies into a grudging willingness to issue an annual Green Card to suitable car-owners who have the temerity to ask for one.

However, make no mistake; insurance companies are the last bastion of the "small print let-out", and the annual Green Card is designed only for drivers who make frequent visits to Europe but who are definitely and beyond question resident in Britain. If you are de facto living in Andorra, or anywhere else beyond the range of a UK FM radio station, any insurance claim you make will almost certainly not be met.

ANDORRAN INSURANCE

The principal difficulty with obtaining Andorran insurance, apart from the possible need to arrange finance to pay for it, is that the policy document will probably be written in Catalan and the company's staff will almost certainly only be able to translate it into either French or Spanish.

So, if your Catalan, Spanish or French are a bit rusty, you might well find that it's easier to get someone else to arrange it for you. Someone, needless to say, who does speak French and Spanish fluently and read Catalan.

This kind of service is provided by a few organisations in Andorra, please refer to the Contacts section at the end of this Report for details of service company Servissim.

REGISTERING A CAR IN ANDORRA

This isn't as easy as you might think, even if you're resident.

First of all, the age of the vehicle is critical. You cannot, under any circumstances, register an imported vehicle in Andorra if it is between three and 25 years old, and there are further problems if it's less than six months old. "Museum vehicles" older than 25 years have restrictions on their use. So in the life of a car you've got only a fairly short period when registration is possible, or an extremely long wait until the car's a pensioner, by which time you probably will be as well, and will have lost interest.

WHY REGISTER YOUR CAR?

However, one has to ask the question – why bother to register it? Certainly the Andorran plates are very attractive, pretty crest and all that, but what exactly do you gain? Not a lot, is the obvious answer.

To take a typical case; you're an English resident with a property in Andorra and you want a vehicle to be left in the Principality for your use during holidays and so on. By far the easiest course of action is to simply buy a cheap, and ideally left-hand drive, car in Britain, take it out to Andorra, stick it in your garage and insure it there. And if you do that, there shouldn't be any problems. If the car is not in Britain, you won't have to pay UK road tax.

NON ANDORRAN-REGISTERED VEHICLES

Technically, you aren't supposed to leave a non Andorran-registered vehicle in the Principality for longer than six months but if you nip down to the market at La Seu d'Urgell in it once every holiday you've probably complied with that rule. And, even if you didn't, it's extremely unlikely anyone would notice unless your chosen car was singularly conspicuous, like a pink Ferrari, and your usual parking space was the main square in Andorra la Vella. And even then, the Andorrans might not do anything about it. Legally, if an originally foreign-registered vehicle is locally registered on tourist plates, it cannot later be sold in Andorra.

REGISTRATION AND TAX

If you do decide to register a vehicle in Andorra, you have to pay a tax or excise duty on first registration. This tax is seven per cent of the notional value of the vehicle, based upon the French trade price guide price for the car, but less the original tax payable in France. This works well for French cars but there can be considerable variations in valuation for vehicles which are not normally sold in France – like virtually all American cars, for instance.

As before, a Service Company can assist with vehicle registration if required. You are most strongly advised to talk to the Company you have chosen **before** making any commitment to buy, as vehicle prices vary widely throughout Europe and the best deal may not necessarily be the obvious deal. Registration will take about three days to complete and the vehicle itself will be needed for about half an hour on the first day.

Don't forget that in Andorra a caravan or trailer has to be registered as a separate vehicle.

TOURIST PLATES

In the last few years, it has become advantageous to register a car on Andorran Tourist Plates. The tax is the same, as in the section above, seven per cent of either the invoice value or the notional value. There is an annual log book and replating fee of 17,000 pesetas. You do not need an address in Andorra but you must supply "an address" outside the country. The plates are recognized throughout the world.

To qualify, vahicles must be less than three years old from date of manufacture, have the correct T2 form (ie the vehicle must have been manufactured within the EC or have the import and transit tax paper issued at the country of original import) and the vehicle's current registration paper must be within 30 days of expiry.

These plates do not, quite obviously, need residence papers to qualify. There are a few minor disadvantages though. The vehicle must be brought back to Andorra every year for replating and cannot be sold on the normal Andorran market unless the seller, or the buyer, pays a further seven per cent of the then notional value. The buyer must, of course, be a resident. However, this is the ideal registration for a PT's vehicles.

You can also buy a resident-plated car and re-register it on tourist plates. This way round you do not have to pay the seven per cent but you will have to when you sell, as above.

BUYING AN ANDORRAN-REGISTERED VEHICLE

First, get your residency, right? Well, nearly right. The rules actually say that you cannot own or buy an Andorran resident-plate vehicle unless you are a resident, and have been for at least six months. However, if some friend, who is a resident, happens to buy a vehicle and then lets you use it, you are not yourself directly involved in either its purchase or ownership. And if you loaned him the money to buy it, and went to the showroom to help him decide on the right color and the type of stereo...

'FIRST LAW OF ANDORRA'

Welcome to the First Law of Andorra – "for every rule, regulation and law there's at least one way round it". Or as one resident puts it: "In Andorra, every cow has two heads."

MULTIPLE VEHICLE OWNERSHIP

This dodge is in common use in Andorra, with the result that the staff of some Service Companies "own" an awful lot of cars! However, please don't expect that you can just march in to one of these companies and more or less demand that they get you an Andorran-plated car because they probably won't.

What is more important to them than your money is the fact that they have to live in Andorra, and it's a very small country. If they "buy" a vehicle for you by the means I've just outlined, they become its legal owner, if not its keeper.

ADVANTAGES AND DISADVANTAGES

You may wish at this stage to consider whether it's really a sensible course of action to hand over several thousand pounds to a man you hardly know to buy himself a car which he may then let you use because that's literally what you're doing. Even worse, he'll charge you an annual fee for the privilege!

From his point of view, if you're the world's worst driver – and that's something you'd have to work at, given the overall standard of the Andorrans – all the parking tickets, speeding tickets, dangerous driving summonses and accident claims are going to be arriving on his doormat, not your's. And that's something he's not going to like, particularly if you don't pay them.

It's also worth noting that if you drive in Andorra, you don't drink, because driving while under the influence of alcohol automatically cancels your insurance cover. And if you haven't any insurance and have an accident, both you and, in this case, the vehicle's "owner" will be in extremely serious trouble.

So this kind of arm's-length purchase is something that needs careful thought, from both sides, and certainly both parties must know and trust each other before embarking on it.

VEHICLE PRICES

Generally, prices for vehicles sold in Andorra are low, especially for four-wheel drive models which are understandably popular because of the terrain. As a fairly typical example, at the beginning of 1991 the top of the range Mitsubishi Shogun sold in the United Kingdom for about £21,000 – the Mitsubishi Pajero or Montero (only the name has been changed – the specification is virtually identical) was available in Andorra for about £12,000, or around 40 per cent less. Of course, it is well known that UK car prices are grossly inflated but even so that's a pretty hefty saving.

The reason for there being two Shoguns in Andorra, virtually identical in all but name, is simply to indicate the country of origin. The Pajero is made in Japan, while the Montero is assembled in Spain and that, apart from very minor variations in specification and retail price, is the only difference between them.

Most vehicle prices in Andorra are competitive, to say the least, but better deals may well be available by buying tax-free for export in other countries, particularly Denmark or Belgium, but the Andorran excise duty should always be remembered and included in your calculations.

Petrol at the time of printing this edition was 85.9 pesetas/litre for supergrade, diesel was 55.6 pesetas /litre. All vehicles more than five years old must pass an annual inspection. The above section on motor vehicles is taken from *ANDORRA – THE UNKNOWN TAX HAVEN* by James Barrington.

SMUGGLING – PAST AND PRESENT

To appreciate the bustling shopping center and tourist destination that is Andorra today, it is important to realise that the first true road linking the main town of Andorra la Vella to Spain was not built until 1929. The paved road to France was completed only in the mid-1930s. Of course, to cross into Spain or France on foot or with a Jeep one does not need roads, mountain paths are still used. Andorrans and their pack mules were for a long time the most active smugglers in Europe. After World War II, benefiting from paved roads to the outside world, most of these contrabandistas became legitimate store-bound merchants, leaving the smuggling of people, drugs, tax-free cigarettes, etc to their visitor-clients!

ANOTHER SECRET: WHERE ARE THE BEST SKI HOTELS?

Once in Andorra, you could do a lot worse than to check in at the L'Isard, 36 Avienda Meritxell (tel: 20092). In the winter, this centrally located hotel caters to the skiers who come for the Pyrenean snows. The L'Isard is on the main street of Andorra la Vella, Avinguda Meritxell. It is a charming place with an old-world atmosphere. In summer the service is just as polite and efficient. Guests in warm weather have the added benefit of using an outdoor pool, the garden, and the tennis court. Very nice rooms with all amenities. Prices start at 4000 pesetas for doubles.

The Hotel Pyrenees, opposite the main branch of Credit Andorra in Andorra la Vella, also comes well recommended. Prices are similar to the Isard.

In the second big town in Andorra, namely Les Escaldes, you will find a variety of comfortable hotels, some quaint and charming, others luxurious and modern. Here are a few to consider:

Hotel Roc Blanc, 5 Placa dels Co-Princeps, Tel: 21486. Although we have been hearing some complaints about this establishment, it does have swimming pool, sauna, gym, garages, tennis courts and a super in-house restaurant, El Pi. Try it and give us your opinion

Hotel Pla, near the top of the Avinguda Carlemany, Tel: 21432. An old tipico inn, said to be founded by some Americans who fought in the Spanish Civil War, located next to a mountain stream and stone bridge. Built in stone. Wrought-iron balconies have French doors, permitting you to step out and look at the dramatic scenery. Elevator. Great dining. Michelin-star potential.

Hotel Cornella, 61 Avinguda Meritxell, Tel: 21480. Close to the bridge that separate the towns of Andorra-la-Vella and Les Escaldes. Garage space for your car is provided. Tasteful lounge, dining room, bar.

Hotel Marfany, 99 Avinguda Carlemany, Tel: 20856. Budget hotel with lots of charm. A well-run French pension. In summer, three meals and a room can be had for less than $20 per day.

The skiing is pretty good with the cheapest lift prices in Europe.

CONFIDENTIAL BANKING IN ANDORRA

Banking is no problem for a non-resident but sometimes communication can be difficult. The only non-residents who cannot open accounts with Andorran banks are the French and Spanish. Even then, they can, with assistance, apply the "First Law of Andorra". As one cannot open a bank account without living in Andorra, yet one cannot obtain immigration permission without having a bank account, this apparent "catch 22" situation can be obviated by having a list of things required to do to live in Andorra. This list should include opening a bank account and when one attends the bank, one shows the banker the list, he then proceeds to open the account as one then has to proceed to the next item on the list which is to apply for immigration.

Banks in Andorra offer a personal and personable service, ie friendly but respectful. Respectful but not smarmy or servile. Bankers are generally competent and positive thinking.

Anything you want to do, just ask. They try hard to make it happen. If they cannot manage it, they are genuinely apologetic. Andorra banks will even receive telex messages and mail for you. They rent you a little private PO Box in the foyer of their banks for your mail! Local banks will serve you well in Spanish, French, Catalan, English, German or Italian (and possibly other languages of which we are not aware). Andorra is no offshore banking centre. Branches and subsidiaries of foreign banks are not permitted. This situation is likely to continue for some time, although a few of the officially "Andorran owned" banks are said to be partly under foreign control (mainly Spanish and French). Write to any of the following banks by name followed by "Principat d'Andorra":

Credit Andorra

Banc Internacional

Banca Mora

Banc Agricol i Comercial

Banca Cassany

Banca Reig

La Caixa

Just ask for "account opening forms in English" or send for them. Credit Andorra is the biggest bank in the country. Credit Andorra will send you a free map and information booklets in English upon request. Some of its major branches are at these adresses:

Avda P Bennloch, 19 Andorra la Vella, Andorra (Tel: 20326)

Avda Carlemany, 42 Escaldes, Andorra (Tel: 20658)

Carretera d'Ordino La Massana, Andorra (Tel: 35169)

Carretera General Saint Julia de Loria, Andorra (Tel: 41021)

Carretera General Ordino, Andorra (Tel: 35030)

No local currency exists. There is de facto use of the Spanish peseta but one has complete freedom to have accounts or conduct transactions in any other currency. No legislation or regulations at all exist on these matters. The banks are all safe. Credit Andorra as we have indicated is the largest, followed by Banc Aricol and by Banc Internacional.

YOUR ANDORRAN BANK ACCOUNT

Walk in off the street to open a bank account in Andorra, and the odds are that you will be asked for a passport and local address. If you don't have both, your initial deposit may be refused. If you come in as a new customer with a suitcase full of cash, you will also be given the cold shoulder. Local banks don't want bad publicity and legal problems abroad resulting from accepting dirty business and thus they turn away potential new customers who don't smell right. But with a reference from a respected local, you will get the red carpet treatment. The outfit we recommend in the Resource section at the end of the book, Servissim, will give you such a reference (and a local address). Just get to know them and show them you are a legitimate person, not involved in drug-dealing or other internationally unsavoury activities such as kiddie porn or slavery.

No one in Andorra gets too excited about people who try to cut corners on their local tax obligations. As there are no taxes in Andorra, tax-evasion is not a crime there, not paying taxes is the natural state of things. But once again, to avoid problems with their closest neighbors, France and Spain, Andorran banks discourage residents or citizens of those two countries from having accounts – unless they have a legitimate excuse – like a home in Andorra or Os. Os is the Secret Spanish Enclave we describe elsewhere in this book.

For those who live in Andorra, it is strongly urged and probably best to have at least two accounts at two separate banks. One account would be a relatively small current account for everyday transactions and pin money. The other is for serious money and investments. Obviously, if you write a check to someone or use a bank credit card, they will know you have funds in Account Number "666" at the "XYZ" bank. Once persons you deal with know your account number, any merchant can figure out your approximate balance by making a computer check for your "credit limit".

The people you deal with are the people you will have problems with. In the event of lawsuits or other problems with someone who knows all about your usual business account, this known account may be frozen or attached (even in Andorra!) under certain circumstances. What circumstances? An Andorra court can freeze or turn over to a plaintiff an identified account where a plaintiff makes a good case that he was (for instance) swindled or defrauded. Interfering with, or even finding out about a secret mother lode account, is another matter. A secret asset management account (not used for check-writing or charge account back-up) in any name is quite private. Such an account in the name of an alternate identity (see PT for comments about a banking passport) is absolutely secure unless your adversary knows your alternate identity and criminal fraud is clearly proved to an Andorran court. Andorra banks do also offer secret numbered accounts but they don't like to talk about them. These accounts are only for known or highly recommended customers and serious money (over £100,000). The owner of any numbered account is only known to and handled by top officers at the bank branch and these accounts are quite confidential – more so, in our opinion, than similar accounts in Switzerland. There, the government can send out a form letter to all banks demanding information about any account that is held in a certain name, or over which a certain named person has signing power. This is not the case in Andorra. Switzerland, by the way, is phasing out numbered accounts and many banks arbitrarily refuse to accept American (USA) clients. Even in Liechtenstein, the minimum starting balance to open a numbered account is US$300,000. What many clients don't realize is that Swiss banks will give up any clients whose names appear on these government forms whether they have a numbered or named account.

Numbered accounts are used to hold and designate investments or fiduciary accounts held for private banking clients in the bank's name. A fiduciary account is simply an account held in another bank. For instance, you want to make a deposit of £100,000 in Andorra. Andorra can put your money into a separate account in a major bank in London. But as far as the London bank is concerned, the owner of that account is the Andorra bank – not you. Such accounts are obviously not usable for normal transactions like check-writing or credit card debits. If you wanted to make a deposit or withdrawal from your fiduciary account, it would have to be via your Andorra bank.

No judge or government official has any right to so much as inquire whether any account is held for Mr So & So except in the event of serious criminal or fraud charges pending against the owner. If a government is the plaintiff and criminal activities are alleged, the local court in Andorra will first determine whether the crimes described are also crimes in Andorra (ie not tax related matters). Even then Andorra has no procedure (as does Switzerland) where a letter goes out to all banks freezing all assets registered in the name of a miscreant. In Andorra, the name of the bank, number of the account and the name of the account holder must both be known. An Andorra court would throw out any legal action that involved claims of tax fraud. As to other matters like divorce disputes, personal injury claims and private civil claims between businessmen, the confidentiality of a numbered account is taken quite seriously and no fishing expeditions would ever uncover such assets – if the bank and account designation was not known. It is, of course, up to the client to ensure that no paper trails lead investigators to such a secret account. Deposits thus would be carefully made either in cash or via third country wire transfers through an impenetrable chain of foreign secret accounts having no links to the depositor.

For absolute confidentiality, the numbered account could be owned by a foreign corporation, a Liechtenstein Foundation or, as suggested in our *PT* book, a new individual created for banking purposes only. Once again, unlike Switzerland, there is no requirement that the "beneficial" or real owner of any account be on record with the bank. For those who have forgotten and don't have *PT-1* handy, creating a new individual would be accomplished by Mr "C" acquiring a second passport in a new name, as Mr "N". The new named individual ("N") is the only account holder known to the bank. Under any circumstance, even an alleged crime, any search for funds owned by Conrad Criminal would not lead to or uncover an account belonging to "N", Norbert Newname. As there are new laws (passed since 1990 when our first Andorra Report was written), to combat "money laundering" by drug dealers or organised crime, any individual directly involved in such activities would be well advised not to have a physical presence in Andorra. **An account alone would probably be safe. But if an individual on the Interpol wanted list was apprehended locally, he would get no protection from the Andorran police** – unless he was an Andorran! Local police are quite tough on foreigners who bring international pressure, disrepute to the banking system or otherwise attract bad publicity to the Andorran banks. The cops could engage in arm-twisting to get an accused international criminal to authorise the disclosure and surrender of his local account. However, if the miscreant is a non-resident, it would be difficult if not impossible for any bank to be forced to give any information about any client or his business with the bank. Having said this, we will also comment that banks do not want to accept bloodstained money from corrupt dictators or deal with the proceeds of crime. Andorrans by and large are a very moral and Catholic people. The bankers hate bad publicity.

Above all, they do not want to have any conflicts or any problems at all with Spanish or French banking or police authorities. These neighbors could inflict a great deal of damage by simply creating a bureaucratic slowdown at the border. Within an hour, traffic in Andorra would be in a gridlock. Accordingly, they generally refuse to open new accounts for individuals who are citizens of or admit to being resident in France or Spain. Aside from that, for years Andorran banks have prospered because, just like Switzerland, they discreetly accepted and managed "black money" from all over the world. Andorran morality is common sense. They have no objection to people who engage in purely technical violations of laws that don't even exist locally. Such things as insider trading, smuggling and tax avoidance are, to them, the normal modus operandi of life. The Andorrans have no legal concept of the Full Money Back Guaranty of Satisfaction. If a company like Scope International wants to offer such a deal (as it does) to their clients, that's fine. But the Andorran Courts will not enforce them. The rule is Let the Buyer Be Wary.

Once a client has a personal relationship with his banker if there was a whiff of trouble, such as a lawsuit being filed in Andorra, the banker could be given, and would follow, standing instructions to wire-transfer all assets to another account somewhere on the other end of the Earth. How to establish such rapport? Easy! See Dr. Hill's other Scope book, *Think Like A Tycoon*. (Review the chapter You & Your Banker for helpful hints). When your assets are threatened, it helps to have friends for damage control.

In one near-legendary case reported a few years back in the British tabloids, an Andorran bank official involved in questioning by Scotland Yard officials, after giving his name, refused to admit that he worked for a certain bank, **or even that the bank existed**. As a result, questions about the account being investigated were never asked.

Accounts in Andorra may be kept in any currency. Interest is about .025 per cent per year below what would be received in the premier banks of the country of the currency held. These are fiduciary accounts, held in the Andorran bank's name in major banks abroad, and the bank's profit is the differential. This is not much to you but it's a golden crumb for them. Enough golden crumbs and you've got a golden cake. The banks will act as a stock-broker and place orders directly for you in their name – or they can open new accounts with a broker you use for futures trading, commodity speculation, or any other form of investment. If you want to keep your ownership of the account confidential, it is obviously best to channel all orders via the bank – even if the bank would agree to give you power of attorney to run this account as "investment advisor" to yourself. The banks will also choose and manage your investment portfolio but in this regard they do not have the successful track record of some of the Swiss banks like Julius Baer or Vontoble Bank. For owning a conservative portfolio of bonds, they are perfectly OK, however.

There is no question that the Swiss banks' services are more professional and efficient. But the Andorra banks try hard. One of our readers wrote this:

"I made several inquiries by letter from London, asking if a certain bond I owned had been sold. Previously, I'd always received a prompt answer to any such questions from the English-speaking bank manager in La Massana. But this time: Silence! I wrote a follow-up letter. No answer. Wondering if something had gone drastically wrong, I finally broke radio silence and called, asking for my man. No one at the other end spoke English and I could not be sure if I had gotten through. I was worried but postponed further inquiries until I went on my usual trip to Andorra to open the ski season. Before visiting the bank I dropped in on the chap you had recommended and asked him to accompany me in case of language problems. Before we went over to the bank, he told me he knew what the problem was. The old, English-speaking manager had transferred banks and no one at my branch now spoke English. Because under the secrecy rules, only the manager could deal with correspondence, she felt she shouldn't talk to someone else (even her superior at main office) but should wait for a personal visit. He picked up the phone and spoke to the manager with whom he had a good rapport. We went over together and I signed a paper authorizing my new agent in Andorra to liaise with the bank manager should such a problem ever arise again. It turned out that as far as my instructions went, they had been executed perfectly. Because the Andorrans have a somewhat unconventional way of thinking, and strange unexpected problems like this often come up, I regard the payment of £550 a year as very cheap insurance to oversee and protect what have become serious assets in Andorra. In a Swiss bank, the officer would have simply had a translation made of incoming and outgoing mail without my name or address being given to the translator. But here, they took the secrecy so seriously that the mere fact a client had unloaded a bunch of dollar bonds was considered a secret the manager felt should go no further".

If you own or are thinking of buying real estate, Servissim can refer you to a lawyer who will form a company (not in Andorra, for reasons explained elsewhere) for you, and it can act as the depository for the company when rent checks come in. Banks can make or guaranty loans to you secured by your own assets on deposit with them (back to back loans) or provide any service offered by any Swiss bank. The fees are always less (often by half) than Swiss charges for similar services.

As to your current, or pin money account, you can write checks in any currency, but forgetting about secrecy, it is still not a good idea to pay small bills in England or the USA with an Andorran check. Why? The receiving bank (ie your creditor's bank) will probably insist that it be handled as a collection item with up to a £30 (or $60) collection and handling charge that will no doubt vastly annoy your creditor. It may also take a month for the check to clear. It would be better to buy a bank draft (in Andorra) on a bank in the place where the debt is due. You can get this draft by mail, phone or fax from anywhere, sent anywhere – once you have an account. Then you mail this bank draft to your creditor. This draft will cost a nominal amount, perhaps £1 or £2. Or you can transfer larger amounts by wire transfer. The cost on this is also nominal although you may pay around £20 for the communication costs.

You can deposit checks, personal or otherwise, in your Andorran bank from anywhere in the world, and the charge by your bank for collecting these checks will be generally under £2.50 ($5). There is no collection charge if the funds are changed into a different currency at the moment of deposit. Collection charges are rolled into the exchange spread. As mentioned, you can have an account in any currency and in any amount. But small current accounts will not pay interest. If you want to exchange currencies, within the account, you get a special exchange rate that including the spread, normally costs you under one per cent (interbank rate) rather than the tourist rate which is closer to six per cent. There is no charge for depositing cash – unlike Switzerland where they will try to nail you for a "counting fee" of around one per cent. Of course good customers in Switzerland can usually get the banks to reduce this to 0.25 of one per cent on larger cash transactions (over $100,000).

There is absolutely no government reporting of any financial transactions except for bank robberies! Due to the one entry and one exit from the country, robbing a bank and getting away with it would be a real challenge in Andorra! It hasn't happened in living memory. As you would expect, there are no tax treaties nor information exchange and disclosure treaties with any other countries. Having said all that, Spain has some leverage and France has even more. Thus individuals potentially on the wrong side of the law in those countries should do business elsewhere. There is one other thing to note, of the six banks in Andorra, one, La Caixa, is essentially a branch of a major Spanish-owned international bank of the same name. Caixa Bank computer terminals anywhere in the world can tap into information on any Andorran account at La Caixa. This may be convenient if you are in their New York branch and want to withdraw a million in cash. It also means that your banking information is less secure there than at any other bank in Andorra. At the other banks, if you have a Visa or Master card that ties into your account, your balance and credit information can probably be obtained by any one of a hundred million merchants or computer hackers or tax authorities. But your secret investment accounts are secret. With La Caixa, tax information treaties between many countries (and Spain) could cause your name to be fed into a computer and out would pop your deep dark Andorra financial secrets.

So, if you want privacy, steer clear of La Caixa. No harm in using it for your current, bill-paying account and credit card link, however. In fact, the international status of this bank may be helpful in using your plastic in cash dispensers abroad. This bank, by the way, is under pressure from the Andorra government to sell out to locals. It is are not allowed to open any new offices nor to expand. But probably it will be around for at least a few more years.

Americans? There are no more than 50 North Americans (including former Americans) resident in Andorra. Financial transactions with the USA are rare. Most IRS agents don't even know it exists.

CURRENCY AND CURRENCY EXCHANGE

The Spanish peseta and French franc are both legal tender throughout Andorra, which has no currency of its own, but the peseta is used more often and can be considered the official currency, as the government uses it for its transactions. Having said that, any currency will be accepted by the banks and property prices, even local mortgages, often are quoted in US dollars, Swiss francs and German marks. Most barmen and shopkeepers will refuse to take anything other than French francs or pesetas when you are stocking up on beer or bread. Prices quoted in francs can be up to five per cent higher than the equivalent in pesetas, with the franc having a slightly worse exchange rate, so it makes sense to use pesetas for small-scale trading.

There is no restriction on currency exchange or any other type of exchange control. Fund transfers can be made to and from any other part of the world, depending on exchange regulations in the other country involved, but PTs know how to get round such trivial details.

CREDIT CARDS

The exchange rate in Andorra for sterling is much better than usually offered in the UK, so it is a good idea for tourists to use credit cards, travellers' checks or Eurocheques on arrival in the Principality. The use of Access and Visa cards gradually is becoming more acceptable, especially at banks, but don't rely on being able to use them for credit universally.

CASH DISPENSERS

PTs who will be equipped with a range of plastic cards are more likely than most to be able to use cash dispensing machines at Andorran banks. Often, a machine will spit out one proffered credit card ungraciously but gratefully accept another card issued by a different company. On the other hand, a different bank's machine may accept the first card offered without question. Banca Mora/Banc Internacional and Banc Agricol machines seem to have the highest success rate with Access and Visa cards. All dispensers offer English for transactions.

THE DINER

Although we said earlier that Andorra has no currency of its own, gold commemorative coins periodically are issued as investments. The diner has various denominations and can be bought in banks.

THE INVISIBLE CHECK – A UNIQUE ANDORRAN INSTITUTION

We would probably call it a bill of exchange, or automatic debit. But it has been around in Andorra for 500 years or more. Suppose you have a home in Andorra or Os. You start to do business with a particular hardware store or you own property needing garbage collection and electricity or you get a telephone. Before any municipal services are delivered, you will be obliged to fill out an application form in Catalan. In the fine print – that you couldn't understand even if it was in **bold type** – this contract signed by you, allows your supplier of goods or services to write what amounts to a check from you to him, and deposit this instrument (called a *Lletre de Canvi*) to his own Andorra account. Your account is then debited. You will not know about it until you get your next financial statement. Your supplier can – by asking if a Lletre de Canvi for a certain amount is good – find out your balance at any time. Of course your statement would show the debit and which supplier charged your account. If any amount is erroneously or fraudulently charged, you can always get the debit adjusted or reversed. If you do not like this standard Andorra arrangement, you can sign a form blocking your account. But if you do that, you may find yourself without any community services or utilities. Why? Because the *Lletre de Canvi* is the way they collect their charges. They refuse to send out bills. Reasoning? Why should they have to wait till you get around to paying? There is no mechanism for paying in advance either. In Andorra, merchants and others customarily use the Lletre de Canvi, just as described, and assume that you will always have the money to pay for any goods or services you've received. If you won't or can't pay local bills promptly, you may find yourself bounced out of the country. As in Switzerland, not settling up your bills promptly with a local merchant is tantamount to a crime. Moral of the story: if you live some of the time in Andorra, you need a current account for such bills at one bank and a secret account at another bank for serious investing.

Using any bank in Andorra, it is possible to obtain credit cards like Visa, Mastercard, American Express, Diner's etc. Charges made on these cards are automatically paid upon presentation to your bank and there is no "credit" extended. Thus strictly speaking, these cards are "debit cards" as your account is debited almost immediately after you use them. There are no charges on the cards aside from the usual small annual fees. For people who live in Andorra, there are strictly local cards (La Clau or Principat) that are very convenient to use because they are accepted by cash dispensers at all local banks and in Spain and on Spanish toll-road automatic charge machines. Further, local stores will give a discount (usually ten per cent) on all purchases made with these cards as you are presumed to be a local resident and repeat customer. The merchants don't pay any charges on these cards either. Most credit card transactions are now done on electronic Point of Sale machines and rarely by the old manual method, so do not try to exceed your credit limit.

SAFETY OF ANDORRAN BANK DEPOSITS

Banks permitted to operate in Andorra are all locally owned with the exception of the Spanish-owned La Caixa. The reason for this one foreign bank is that La Caixa (now with a substantial minority of local ownership) came in before the laws prohibited any foreign banks from opening branches or subsidiaries in Andorra. All the banks are members of a cartel or monopoly with an agreement among themselves and the government that if any bank failed, the others would protect their depositors. As all the banks are run conservatively and as it is essentially a criminal offense to go bankrupt (same as in Switzerland), it is almost unthinkable that any Andorra bank would fold under present circumstances. Still, we wouldn't advise investors to keep all eggs in one basket, nor even in one country. Venerable institutions, and even whole nations, all disintegrate sooner or later. Here are the names of the Andorra banks and the number of branches each has:

Credit Andorra 13, Banca Mora/Banc Internacional 11, Banc Agricole i Commercial 8, Banca Cassany 6, Banca Reig 5, La Caixa thousands of offices worldwide.

La Caixa should not be confused with Caixa Andorana de Seguretat Social or CASS. This is a government-sponsored group health insurance and pension plan. More about this in the next chapter.

HEALTH INSURANCE IN ANDORRA

If you have a work permit in Andorra, you have no choice but to join the health insurance scheme. All persons legally working are **automatically enrolled** in the CASS plan. It covers all job-related injuries and any other health problems.

Medical care is excellent and several of the many physicians in town speak English. Your employer will pay part of the premium and your bank account will be debited for the balance.

If you are a PT who spends time in Andorra but do not have a work permit nor a residence card, then you have no choice either, you **cannot** join. If you have a residence permit you have the option of joining, which is advisable since the new law on immigration insists that you must either join CASS or have a suitable private insurance policy. You can join after the age of 65 in certain circumstances. The following comments are thus aimed at those individuals who have the option.

A service company will help on most medical and health insurance matters, including eligibility and procedures for joining CASS.

SHOULD YOU JOIN?

Couple (both partners) under 65, living at least six months per year in Andorra: Probably yes as (at about £100 per month) it will be just about the cheapest full coverage medical insurance you can get – especially if you have children under 18 who are also automatically covered at no extra charge. After minimum 15 years of membership and age 65, you pay no more premiums but medical coverage continues and you get a nice inflation-adjusted pension check each month besides. You can join at 64, pay for 15 years, and then you get free coverage and your pension. But financially, the best deal falls into place if you (the man of the house) are under 50.

Single individual young and healthy with a good medical plan and no need for a small pension check. Forget it – especially if you don't spend too much time in Andorra. If you need attention outside Andorra or France, getting your reimbursement involves some hassle. For a fuller explanation of the health program and much other useful info, see another £60 book called *Andorra,* by James Barrington. Refer to Resource List in back of book.

TO BE OR NOT TO BE A RESIDENT – THAT IS THE QUESTION

Many people believe that you must have a legal residence somewhere. A PT knows this isn't true. It is possible, even desirable, for those with substantial assets to float around unrecorded on any computers and unmemorized on any ledgers.

You can be a Permanent Tourist. As such you can flit around free as a bird, or you can stay in one nest for all of your life – without ever getting on any official registers. A friend of the author's has been in Switzerland for 38 years as a PT. Another has been in the United States for 45 years.

In Andorra, the letter of the law is that you must register with the new *Cens d'Estrangers* or Foreigners' Census after you have lived continuously in the country for more than three months. However no one checks when you came in or left. There are no border controls nor passport stamps (other than souvenir stamps) given out by Andorra. Further, if you insist upon being a Boy Scout, to comply with the letter of the law, you simply drive across the border (or even go to Os) every three months. Come back and presto! You are a legally landed tourist for another three months. The attractions of nearby Toulouse or Barcelona would probably cause you to leave Andorra every few weeks even if it were not legally required. But fact is no one gives a hoot if you drive across any borders or not. There are no police officers who have "illegal immigrants" as their portfolio. The Andorran cops view their duty as preventing violence, frauds and offenses against Andorrans. Perhaps up to 50 per cent of the foreigners who live in Andorra more or less permanently are not registered. If they do nothing to upset the locals, they are left alone. No one really knows how many foreigners live in Andorra without permits because no one keeps track. But we'd observe there are apartments and homes with room for around 200,000 people and only 25,000 or so are registered.

ADVANTAGES OF BEING REGISTERED

You can exchange your present driving license for a lifetime Andorran license with no test except for Americans whose government has refused a reciprocal deal with Andorrans. USA citizens have to take the test but this might be waived if you knew the local cop. In fact life can run very smoothly in Andorra if you are on good terms with someone in authority – or if you have a local friend in that position. You can register your plane or boat or put your tax-free car on permanent Andorra plates. The negative here is that required Andorra car insurance is just about the most costly outside Tokyo. You can join the national health and pension plan (CASS), discussed in another chapter. If you need to convince another country that you are resident in

Andorra, they can't deny you non-resident status in their country when you have the official paperwork from Andorra in hand. But note however, residence is not domicile and Great Britain, for instance, would probably still hit your Estate in England for estate/inheritance taxes. If Andorra should ever tighten up on immigration and residence, those already registered would be "grand-fathered" in but unregistered property owners might be forced to leave. In Switzerland, a few years back, property owners who lived in their homes full time with "tourist status" became monitored so that now they can live in their homes no more than three months per year. Obviously, my PT friend who has been in the same Swiss apartment for most of his life follows the basic PT rule and rents! You'd have the right of appeal if any policeman or other official told you to leave the country. If non registered, you'd have to leave.

DISADVANTAGES OF BEING REGISTERED

Your whereabouts, background and assets are known to a potential Big Brother. If the Socialists take over, if rules change or if income taxes are ever imposed, your goose is cooked. This is more than likely in the 21st Century because there will eventually be great pressure upon Andorra to join the EC and conform to its norms. Probably, you've got another 50 years. So don't lose any sleep over major changes being made next week. There is no chance that under present arrangements you'd ever get a passport although any child born in Andorra to you (if you were registered) could become a citizen after 18 years of continuous residence. Of course if Andorra becomes a full member of the EC -because it offers all kinds of subsidies – Andorra would probably have to give anyone who'd been a legal resident for more than five years their citizenship. You would be subject to a small tax (around £200 p/a) or service charge for municipal services as the head of a household. If you own property, you are also subject to about half of this tax whether registered or not. The Andorrans require that you be registered with your home country's nearest consulate as a resident. They will also want a "no-convictions" certificate. You must own a property and have a substantial local bank balance. Renting will not do any more. The one exception would be in cases where an Andorran employer certified you as a necessary individual in his business. Then you could rent.

So, back to the question. Should you become a legal resident? The answer is "It depends on you". Some people like to "belong" and the actual monetary cost of belonging and actually living there full time is pretty cheap in Andorra – perhaps the lowest cost in the world for a wealthy person.

This author feels that for a PT, the answer in Andorra or any other tax haven is clearly "Not to belong". The only exception being exceedingly rare cases. For instance: you are Danish or a tax-exile from some other Socialist Paradise, and your home country refuses to renew your passport unless you prove you are either an income taxpayer in Denmark or living as a legally registered foreigner and paying at least some taxes in some other country. In such case, to keep your passport current, you'd need to register as a resident of Andorra and file copies of those papers with your Consulate. [Author's personal note: If I were a citizen of such a country as Denmark, I'd quickly acquire another passport rather than put up with such invasions of my privacy.] For the Dane or Swede who doesn't want to give up his passport, it might be appropriate to register in Andorra as a resident.

This author would rather be invisible; a citizen of a country which doesn't care about him nor keep track of him once he's left; physically present in a country that is safe, tolerant, and leaves him alone. Andorra fills the latter requirement and is thus a top choice for a PT. The only disadvantage is that the country is, like Switzerland, a cold place to be in the winter. This is great if you like winter sports, the topic of another chapter.

HOW TO BOOK YOUR HOTEL

With more than 35,000 hotel rooms, 26 camping sites and 250 restaurants, the tourism infrastructure offers the visitor a wide choice.

To help Andorra's visitors, a truly advanced computer service is continually receiving and channelling out information relative to Andorra. There are terminals in all the information offices in each Parish in Andorra, nine in total. Terminals are also found in the Andorra tourist offices in London, Berlin, Paris, Barcelona and Meise, Belgium.

A computer answers visitors' questions related to basic information about the country. From "what to do in Andorra" to "how to get to" a given place. "No one", the tourist office states, "knows more facts about the principality than our computer".

SPORTSMAN'S PARADISE

Despite its small number of inhabitants, Andorra nevertheless offers a great variety of sporting activities. The proficiency level of Andorrans is quite professional in some of these activities. Shooting, particularly clay pigeon shooting, has even acquired a certain international prestige. Andorrans regularly take top prizes.

Dressage, riding, tennis, basketball, mountaineering, swimming, rugby and athletics have a good following, too, with a fair number of participants and spectators.

Football (called soccer in the USA) is the national sport. Naturally it has many near fanatic enthusiasts. Everyone follows inter-town matches with great interest, rejoicing whenever the local team scores.

There is a lot of enthusiasm for motorized sports. Trophies are avidly contested. Motorbike cross country races, hill climbs, and sports-car rallies abound. Clubs and teams keep up the Andorrans' spirits and determination. There is an ever-increasing participation in motorized sports.

One of the most common things in Andorra is snow. In Andorra, though, snow is by no means another word for cold. Brilliant sunshine is always sure to bring a warm note to an idyllic excursion by sled or sleigh – or a cross country skiing trip up in the mountains. Snowbikes are popular. Snowbiking is a sport with a large number of enthusiasts attracted by its beauty as a spectacle; the emotion and adventure of cutting a path through sheets of virgin powder at high speeds.

The ski stations in the Principality of Andorra are: Pas de la Casa-Grau Roig, Soldeu-Tarter (a favorite with young girls), Arinsal, Pal and Arcalis.

SKIING AND WINTER SPORTS IN ANDORRA

Twenty years ago the only reason Londoners went to Andorra was for the cheap package ski holidays. The cost of lodging, eats, lift-passes and especially apres ski entertainment and booze was the cheapest in Europe. Equipment and lodgings in those days was a bit makeshift and primitive, and the instruction certainly wasn't AAA.

Now things have changed! Prices are still bargain basement but the quality of everything has gone up dramatically. Slopes have been professionally graded. Artificial snow, made by spraying water cannon at night, keep the slopes well covered with a good base for longer seasons. Lift equipment with few exceptions is of very recent vintage and is first rate. The instructors and ski-schools have gone from C+ in the old days to A rated today. Many instructors are British or English speaking. Ski equipment and clothes are available in incredible variety and at a considerable discount from prices everywhere else.

Why should any skier go elsewhere? Aside from the fact that most people get in their cars and go to the closest slopes, there are some skiers who wouldn't like Andorra. For starters, Andorra is now one of the most popular places in Europe. If skiers go to other places it is because the runs in Andorra are mainly for beginners and intermediates. For more death-defying leaps and killer slopes Switzerland is better. Also for snob appeal, at five times the price, you can't beat St Moritz or Gstaad. The beautiful international people go to those places. Ordinary blokes and dollies go to Andorra. You might not meet Sean Connery but there are plenty of middle class folks who swear by Andorra. Because of the cost of the equipment, trip and lift passes, it is not for Poverty Pete. There are a few young ski-bums of both sexes who own nothing more than their jeans, parka and skis. They work any night job they can get at resorts and get free passes. They live only for skiing. Some turn out to be champions or top-notch ski instructors. Normally kids are full time in this "profession" for a year or three until they find it necessary to move into something more substantial. Skiers, like yacht people, tend to be "well off", friendly, well mannered, and easy to get to know.

As any unattached male knows, there is no better way for a guy who can ski a bit than to offer free lessons to a snow bunny (female beginner). Thus, due to the presence of thousands of students, secretaries, dental assistants and such, the slopes of Andorra become positive sex havens during the season from around 15 December to 1 March, and absolute heaven during the crowded Christmas vacation and other school breaks. Waiting for your gondola or chair-lift becomes "getting acquainted time". Here is the rundown on the major ski areas:

ARINSAL. Nearest to La Massana a town that is largely English. Big car park in the village with chair-lift to the slopes. Excellent for beginners with many levels of classes in a highly regarded ski school. There are 15 lifts, around 30 km of runs. The height of runs is about the same in all the ski resorts at 2,800 metres (highest) to 1,550 (lowest).

PAL: A slightly longer drive (only ten minutes more) from La Massana than Arisinal, less crowded on the higher runs, best views, 35 km of runs. Fewer ski bunnies, less emphasis on lessons, better solo skiing for the intermediate.

ARCALIS: Least crowded, preferred by the locals, most difficult runs, seldom has lift-lines. Due to north-facing slopes, more powder, less sun and less melt. Magnificent views. Takes longest to get to by car from La Massana but we are only talking about 30 minutes.

THE BIG TWO (SKI RESORTS)

Pas de La Casa/Grau Roig. These two adjacent resorts are just off the main highway, close to the French border. This makes them attractive to French day-skiers. They are also favorites on the package tour itinerary. Also, they are by far the biggest in the area with some 50 lifts and 100 km of fine runs. At peak times, like Christmas week, you will spend far more time in queues than skiing. But if you are there mainly for the socializing, that's OK. If you book via a travel agent, this is probably where they will send you. You should probably get a combined lift-pass if you will be there for a week or more.

Soldeu/El Tartar. Also off the main highway, closer to Spain, with 60 km of runs. What we said about the above also goes for these places. Nothing wrong with them at all. They are just bigger, more commercial and impersonal than the other, smaller resorts we have mentioned. As with brands of beer, each place has its adherents. It will be up to you to visit all the resorts and choose your own personal favorites.

General Hints. To get more time skiing, and less time waiting, avoid week-ends and peak periods if possible. Buy snow chains for your car as soon as you get to Andorra. They are required and will be urgently needed if you get stuck in a snowstorm. Negotiate for a better room rate than you are first offered unless the place is offering you its last room and there are plenty of others in line behind you waiting to get it. Get a season ticket to all lifts in Andorra if you will be there for a whole season.

Don't gamble, at least in any public place. Even small money betting on card games or pool could cause problems. Getting into fist-fights or physical confrontations, especially with Andorrans, is likewise not a good idea.

Walk away from problems. Being taken into custody by Andorran cops is not an experience you will treasure.

Don't do drugs in any public place. Frame ups are unheard of but recreational hard and soft drugs are illegal and its best to stay out of trouble in a foreign country.

OTHER SPORTS

Indoor. If you want to visit one of the **best gyms in the world**, it will cost about £14 for the day to visit the **Anyos Sports Centre**. Go in with a member and it will be about half price. Or if you live in Andorra you could join on a permanent basis for around £250 per year.

Here's what you get: saunas, sun-tanning, three hot-tubs (Jacuzzi), weightlifting and muscle building equipment, gymnastics, Olympic shooting range, golf simulators, huge indoor heated swimming pool, indoor tennis and squash. Instruction in all of the above plus many classes from aerobics to martial arts.

Ice skating. Visit the Ice Palace (Palau de Gel) at Canillo.

Picnics and hiking are especially pleasant in Andorra as all the land is public outside of built up areas. You can feel free to drink from the many mountain streams at the higher altitudes. There are said to be more species of wild mountain flowers in Andorra than anywhere else on earth. Please don't pick them. Only light fires where it will be safe ie where there is clear evidence of long use of a fire-site, and don't leave your garbage behind. There are forest rangers known as Banders, and like the cops, will never cause you any trouble if you behave yourself. But start shooting the birds, building dangerous fires or making a mess and you may find yourself with a major fine.

Equestrian activities. Horses and ponies can be hired near the Casa Nono Restaurant recommended in the Restaurant Section.

Mountain biking. A popular but strenuous activity. Plenty of trails.

Fishing for mountain trout. Get permits, maps, tackle and advice at any of the many sport shops downtown, or better still at the Sindicat d'Iniciativa, Placa Rebes (the square in the centre of town next to the main communal car park). They speak English there and can explain the rules and areas available. You might also like to see the government trout hatchery at El Serrat.

Hunting and shooting. You will need a license and a gun permit to hunt the mountain goat. This is the local trophy. But the season is only one week and the odds that you'll get one are slim. If these animals are shot out of season these days, the fine may be set at levels to bankrupt you. Better to join a gun club and shoot skeet (clay pigeons). You will have good instruction and formidable competition as native Andorrans are regular winners and finalists in international shooting competitions. As you leave La Massana there is one of the more unique target ranges in the world with shooters on one side of the public road and the targets on the other. It is said they haven't downed a driver yet. For more info on hunting and competition contact local sport gun shops.

ANDORRA: HISTORY

How did this little principality keep its independence from the neighboring major nations of France and Spain?

The first known written reference to Andorra is to be found in a text of Polibi, a 2nd century BC Roman. His narrative tells how the Andorrans with the long-gone Aranese and Berguedans confronted and were pushed aside by Carthaginian troops who passed through the Pyrenees on their way to invade Italy. Carthage's army under Hannibal was defeated by the Romans and then the Andorrans were left alone.

A lot of small-time battles for independence were then fought on an on and off basis for the next 1,000 years, first with the legions of the Roman Empire, then Visigoths and finally the Moors. Because of its isolation and poverty, Andorra always paid some tribute and was "under" a major power but usually stayed autonomous. Basic stuff, really, but all the battles with foreign invaders helped to knit the Andorrans together as a community. In 843, the Emperor, Charles the Bald, so called because his hairstyle was not unlike that of your author, granted his Andorran valleys to Count Sunifred I of neighboring Cerdanya-Urgell. From the 11th century, the Bishops of Urgell gradually increased their power until they gained Andorra as the result of bequests and rights granted or ceded by the Counts of Urgell to the Church. Later, hostility shown by neighboring lords led the Bishop of Urgell to seek the military protection of the powerful French House of Cabot, to whom Andorra was feudalized.

At the end of the 12th century, love was to change the course of history for the tiny mountainous enclave known then, as now, as the Valls d'Andorra or the Valleys of Andorra. Arnalda Cabot married Viscount Arnau of Castellbo. Subsequently their only child, the stunningly beautiful Ermessenda married the Count of Foix, Roger Bernat II, who had been born in France in 1208. They insisted that Andorra was theirs alone and part of France which he was destined to rule. Andorra for a short time was a center of conflict. What does this have to do with you? Patience!

Violent clashes between the Spanish Bishops of Urgell and the French Counts of Foix were brought to an end under the arbitration of Pere II of Catalonia by means of agreements known as *Pareatges*. Two of these were drawn up, in 1278 and 1288. Essentially, these documents created a dual monarchy with the Bishop of Urgell and the Count of Foix made joint Princes and then collecting the feudal tithe on alternate years, while day-to-day matters were to be handled by a locally elected council.

The signing of these arbitration acts marked the birth of the present political regime. They are still the basic constitution in Andorra today. These laws are followed by a parliament created in 1419 and now called the *Counsell de la Terra*.

The Principality of Andorra is thus the oldest continuously surviving sovereign state in Europe. Note: The Isle of Man has an older local legislature but the Queen of England is the sovereign. These islands are autonomous, but not independent. Andorra still preserves traditional institutions inherited from the Middle Ages. The Andorran political system is still based on the regime of co-princedom (how we like that word!) dating from the signing of the *Pareatges*. Today, the President of France (or the Count of Foix if he ever returns to power as the King of France) and the Bishop of Urgell are symbolic co-sovereigns but as they have bigger fish to fry, they have always let the anarchists [anarchists believe in minimum government and local autonomy] in the Andorran Parliament run things. The French president and the Spanish prelate never sit in their symbolic vacant throne in parliament. But their pictures are displayed in City Hall. Since neither "Prince" has clear control, Andorra is free of Big Brother. France acts for Andorra in matters of foreign policy but the Prince-Bishop retains his power of veto, ensuring Andorra's best interests are served. Both France and Spain largely ignore Andorra.

Although there are 14 political parties none of these are political in the recognized sense and only native Andorrans are allowed to vote in general elections. Not a monarchy or democracy, Andorra is the only true "anarchy" on earth where maximum individual freedom reigns supreme.

The modern age is limping into this sanctuary in the Pyrenees. Not long ago the incorporation into the judicial system of a public prosecutor and the novel concept of a defence lawyer was authorized. We have yet to see if mountain people can adjust to a modern legal system or if the new fangled judicial system, as we suspect, will simply not be used much.

REAL ESTATE: PICTURESQUE CHALETS, £150,000

Finding a place to live in Andorra is easy. It is also relatively cheap. Andorra housing is priced way below that of Monaco, Sark, Campione, Gibraltar, Bermuda and the rest. This said, you can find still cheaper homes in Spain, Portugal or rural France. But they are not in a pure tax-haven where Big Brother will stay out of your life. According to *The International,* retired Lloyds Bank executive Roger Goodale and his wife Tina arrived in Andorra a few years ago. [Free subscriptions to this interesting monthly magazine for PTs are available to Hill Report readers upon application to The International, Greystoke Place, Fetter Lane, London EC4A 1ND, United Kingdom]. Aside from being amazed by the local banking community's efficient service, Roger Goodale marvelled at the relatively low cost of housing. He bought a modern three-bedroom flat, high above the village of Anyos with a view to kill for. The price? £65,000.

"We decided to settle in Andorra because property is relatively cheap and we pay no tax. We've had no immigration problems and, what's more, Andorra is politically stable and the locals are very friendly," said Mr Goodale, who is now deceased.

Home prices start at around £150,000. Now maybe is the time to buy. A 10 per cent to 15 per cent yearly increase in real estate is not uncommon in the more sought-after parts of

Andorra. No major slump in the market there, although prices were flat in 1992-93. In this writer's opinion they will be playing catch up for many years to come. Why? Because prices are at least two-thirds below those in other tax havens. There are NO restrictions of ANY sort on buying property. Andorrans practise laissez-faire. This has been a model country to prove that a market driven, totally unregulated economy works best. When outsiders tell the Andorrans that Andorra should have more rules, more socialism and more state interference, the Andorrans just smile politely and may ask: "What did an intrusive government do for you? What kind of model can YOU show us?" Socialists have had nothing but dismal economic failure. The longest, roughest and most painful path from capitalism to capitalism is called socialism. Andorra so far wants none of it.

TAXES IN ANDORRA

There is no direct taxation of individuals. Period. No income tax, no capital gains, no gift tax, no capital transfer tax, no inheritance tax, no estate tax, and no wealth tax. There is no value added tax.

Where do they get money to build roads, fund schools, and pay for police and courts?

IMPORT DUTY

The main source of revenue is an *Impost de Consum* of one per cent on food and drinks (including alcohol), a four per cent duty on almost everything else, a seven per cent tax on perfumes, most electronic items, and musical instruments. There is a 12 per cent duty on luxury items such as fur coats and jewelry. There are also specific taxes that can be quite high, such as 60 per cent on pipe tobacco and 19 per cent on whisky. But since alcohol and tobacco are taxed at as much as 2,000 per cent in some countries, the result is that the price of liquor and cigarettes is still less than anywhere else in Europe.

Other revenues will come from a new tax of around £4 million per annum shared by the cartel of banks, and another proposed tax of ten per cent on electricity and phone bills.

LOCAL TAXES (BETTER CALLED SERVICE CHARGES)

Property owners and registered residents are charged by their local community for municipal services such as street lights, garbage collections and street maintenance. Each *comu* establishes its own rate but the following would be a typical bill for a year:

Millionaire's Tax Bill in Andorra	*Example only*
Foc i Lloc (hearth and home) pesetas	6,000
(exempt if over 65)	
Property owner 10,000 ptas for apartment or	
17,500 for chalet	17,500
Note: There are additional charges (small) for other members of	
a household (assume one)	2,750
Car road tax ranges from 2,200 to 11,000	11,000
Communal tax: property owner	
Flat 12,000, chalet 24,000	24,000
Annual tax bill for a mythical typical couple occupying a top-of-the-market chalet worth £275,000 (assuming three-bedroom, three-bath home with most expensive BMW in the garage)	**Pesetas 61,250**

Although exchange rates fluctuate widely with a 40 per cent or more variability from the figures below, just to have some idea of the costs in your home currency, we use the following arbitrary exchange rate for this example and throughout this book:

£1= FF10 French francs= $1.80 USA dollars= 180 pesetas **Total for one year's registered residence in Andorra: 61,250 This is equal to about $612 or £340 or Fr 3400 per annum regardless of whether your income is £25,000 per year or £25 billion.** How does this bill stack up against your present annual gift to your government?

OTHER POSSIBLE TAXES

When a property is constructed, bought or sold, there are taxes based upon the size of the property. Figure around two per cent of the cost of the property as an "add on". We note that most tax havens have a similar charge when real estate is bought or sold. This is not so bad considering there are no other taxes, like capital gains.

At the time of going to press, the new law on immigration specifies new charges to non-employed resident foreigners but as yet no figures have been decided. There will be an annual payment for the Residence Permit and premiums for education if you have children who go to school. These, it is estimated, are going to be fairly modest, SERVISSIM expects a maximum total of 250,000 pesetas. Up-to-date figures will be available through SERVISSIM as soon as there is an official decision.

HOW TO BUY PROPERTY

Use a local consultant like Servissim to help you. [see next chapter.]

Mortgages, if required, can usually be arranged with one or more of the local banks for a period of up to five years or ten years depending on the type of property. Balloon or lump sum loans (interest only) are common.

Large construction companies put together their own financing in co-operation with British and French companies. It is possible to get a 20 year self-amortising mortgage this way. If you are prepared for a do-it-yourself project, contacting French lenders can get you a 20 year, 80 per cent mortgage on almost any property. But you will probably pay from 15 to 20 per cent per annum in interest on a French franc loan. If you have assets or property elsewhere, check and see if your own bank can guarantee your loan or otherwise arrange for a lower than usual interest rate. British banks, in particular Lloyds and Barclays, have made many loans against local properties.

A non-Andorran may not purchase more than $1000m^2$ of land or one private dwelling under Public Title. This figure is per person, it applies to married couples jointly, whether the spouse is on the deed or not but children over 18 are treated separately. There is (First Law of Andorra!) no restriction on properties held under private contract.

PROPERTY TITLES

Properties in Andorra can be transferred by private contract (*Escriptura de Venda* or *Escriptura de Promesa de Compra-Venda*) or be granted a public title (*Escriptura Publica*). New laws introduced in February 1992 restrict the granting of a public title to properties which have a garage or parking space. Existing public titles may be kept, even if the property does not comply, but no public titles will be approved for new properties which do not include individual ownership of a garage or parking space. All of this means properties without a public title will sell at a larger discount than previously.

All valid property transactions must take place in front of one of the two Notaries. These should be either in the form of a private contract written by the Notary or a public title, also drawn up by the Notary. Beware of, or take the best possible advice on, any contract where it is drawn up by the estate agent and then taken to the Notary for "protocolization". These latter contracts might not be valid in law if there is ever alawsuit between you, the former owner or neighbors.

EXISTING AND FUTURE DEVELOPMENT

The speed of building development in Andorra can be expected to slow as a result of the recession and because the principality is running out of usable land. At present, legislation sets a limit of eight per cent on the amount of land to be used for home building and only about two per cent is left; much of that is difficult to develop, needing roads, main services and major earth works. New homes built on this land will be much more expensive than existing property.

Changes in building regulations will also lead to increased costs since the Andorrans decided to halt the rash of hideous concrete blocks which began mushrooming across the valleys in the 1970s. There are restrictions on the size, situation and appearance of all new properties.

YOUR ANDORRA ADDRESS & MAIL-DROP

After much searching for a reliable, well established outfit in Andorra, we recommend **Servissim**, a company offering special terms to Hill Report readers:

Full confidential mail, phone and fax receiving/forwarding service with same day turnaround. Expenses such as postage, Federal Express/DHL or phone/fax costs are billed separately at cost. This service is for individuals only, not companies. If commercial use is intended, discuss in advance.

These Exclusive Reports (worth a substantial part of the annual membership) at no extra charge:

Summary of the New 1993 Constitution (12 pages) and the Implications for Foreigners;
Summary of the New 1993 Law on Immigration;
Summary of the new 1993 Rental Law;
How to get Residence & Work Permits (Step by Step);
Joining the Automobile Club of Andorra;
Joining Andorran Health & Social Security System;
How to Register as a Resident at your local Commune;
For potential apartment owners: Co-proprietor and Condo Ownership;
Obtaining Firearms Permits;
Property Insurance in Andorra;
How to get Vehicle & Driving Licenses in Andorra;
Forming a Company/Doing Commercial Business;
Renting Out Property – Local Rules, Regulations & Customs;
Confidential Banking in Andorra, Information Not Generally Known;
Wills, Estate and Tax Implications for Foreigners;
Local Lingo Lessons (Catalan) & other Fascinating Information on a complimentary 80-minute audiotape.

Unlimited personal assistance and consultations in Andorra including:

*Items marked are charged at standard rates with substantial discount. Requests for those marked * must be made in person.*

* Help obtaining residence;

* One free letter or telephone consultation on any aspect of Andorra before arrival;

* Trouble-free assistance in opening a confidential Andorran bank account;

* Assistance in arranging for a high-security, absolutely confidential communication relay service (in-house or independent private boxes);

Local business consultancy and unrivalled local contacts;

Assistance in registering your car, boat, etc in Andorra (discuss before arriving);

Assistance in finding and renting or buying ( ) suitable property. Servissim is not a real estate broker and receives no commissions on sales. Its advice is objective and probably will save you money. It can also manage rental property, supervise building projects, handle repairs and improvements, guide any project through the local bureaucracy, and obtain building permits. If large amounts of time are expended in this regard, such work will be billed at a reasonable hourly rate.

* Emergency assistance of any kind* – including obtaining local currency on holidays, exchange out of hours – medical problems –legal problems – translations to and from English into most languages and on the spot translation services covering all western European languages;

Hotel recommendations and reservations, car rentals, airport pick-up taxi, charter and helicopter flights;

An exclusive monthly **Letter From Andorra** giving information and news for PTs – not available elsewhere, plus immediate updates on above information sheets;

Personal guided tour of Andorra by SERVISSIM staff.

The PT may be able to achieve **substantial tax and other advantages** by establishing an official residence (for which owned property is needed) or the equivalent for most purposes (for which only a rental address or the address-service is needed). Servissim can guide and assist, depending upon your particular requirements.

To establish your membership, merely mail the first annual fee of £400, giving *The Andorra Report* as reference. Checks payable to ''Servissim SL'' can be in any currencyto the equivalent rate in sterling.

The cost is £400 or equivalent for the first year, reducing to £300 thereafter, which represents a big reduction on the previous cost. Not only have we negotiated even better terms but there has been a considerable peseta devaluation. The dollar rate is subject to exchange fluctuations but at the time of going to pressis US$640 for the first year and $480 thereafter. If you would like to know Servissim better before or after joining, feel free to visit its office in Andorra on ''main street'' opposite Pyrenees department store. Or, send £10 (to cover postage and handling), for an 80-minute cassette tape *Welcome to Andorra*, and other materials on Andorra and Servissim.

Servissim SL, Roc Escolls 3, 4A, Avinguda Meritxell 20, Andorra la Vella, Principat d'Andorra (via France) or, if you prefer, to either Box 133, Credit Andorra or Box 133, Banc Agricol, both in Carretera General, La Massana, Principat d'Andorra (via France). If dialling from France, dial code 628; if dialling from Spain, dial code 9738; if dialling internationally, dial either code +33-628 (via France or +34-738 (via Spain) and then number 60414 or 61148. By fax, use the same codes and the number is 63797.

RENTING IN ANDORRA

Furnished or unfurnished flats plus quite a few houses are always available for rent. Look for them by asking at local bars, or contact Servissim. As a rule, unfurnished accomodation must be taken on a lease of at least one year. But you can get out of most leases by finding a substitute tenant. With the new laws, renting for longer than three months to a non-resident is not allowed, but Servissim is considering how the new regulations square with the "First Law of Andorra". Leasing is a good idea – especially if you are new to Andorra. It gives you time to know the local real estate market. As any tycoon will tell you, the only way to make good deals is to know the local prices well. Strike at the bait only when a real bargain comes along. Distress property, on sale due to divorces, probates, sudden moves, can be acquired once you have made local contacts and start to sniff around.

Furnished flats can be rented for short periods. These tend to be more expensive. Also, they must be booked ahead for the summer season and over Christmas and Easter. Rent starts at about £200 monthly for an unfurnished studio, £400 if furnished. You **will** need a car to get around.

Daily domestic help (Spanish) runs close to £4 an hour. Labor is plentiful though you'll have to import live-in domestics from Spain or Portugal.

Fully furnished studio apartments can be purchased for as little as £40,000. Cut that price by half if you are willing to live in a basement or very undesirable location with no view. Such a dump might be good for establishing a "bona fide" residence cheaply. There is always a demand for cheap rentals if you want to play landlord. Fully furnished two-bedroom flats in modern apartment blocks with heated indoor swimming pools are priced from £75,000. At the top end of the market, a dynamite four-bedroom, two-bathroom free standing chalet with multi-car parking, vast gardens and a view can be found for around £400,000 Sterling.

Returns on rented out service apartments can be as high as a tax free eight per cent net, although the market is fluctuating due to the recession and shortage of suitable tenants. One particular project – the Anyos Aparthotel – guarantees management and a six per cent net per annum cash return with capital appreciation at eight to ten per cent per annum. But, beware, guarantees are always good until there are market reverses. A guarantor usually fails at the only time you'd need him! We are not knocking this deal. Just be aware that no one is going to give you a free lunch. There are always risks.

Servissim has come up with Andorra's first fully-secured, taz-free, rental property bond. Instead of owning your own rental property, with all the individual risks attached, it offers a co-ownership – definitely NOT a timeshare – Participation Fund in which bondholders jointly own the properties, the income and the capital growth, thus sharing the risks. The total income/ growth is calculated at 12 per cent per annum and bonds are fixed for a minimum of 30 months. The minimum investment is around ££2,500 (US$4,000), and they are tax-free bearer bonds ie discreet. A detailed brochure is available from Servissim. The difference with this scheme is that you are not tied to one property and entry and exit, therefore, is much easier. Of course, the same cautions must apply as above.

BUILD YOUR OWN CHALET?

Building your own house in Andorra is quite a task since local councils all specify the exact details of almost everything having to do with the **exterior**. For instance, all Andorran houses must have walls clad with planked wood or a local rough exterior stone. In some parts of Andorra, only chalets built in the style of old stone barns with 25cm rough granite walls are accepted. In other parts, the local councils will even decide the degree of your roof's slant. These strict aesthetic regulations do tend to give the valley a "rustic" look. Thus ambience is preserved better in an anarchy than in other places.

We suggest that you don't play general contractor or do-it-yourself builder unless you are very experienced and are willing to follow local guidelines.

HOW TO GET RESIDENCE & WORK PERMITS

Already some 1500 United Kingdom expatriates and tax refugees, "too rich to die in London and too poor to live in Monaco" are resident in Andorra.

Paperwork involved is not as easy as it used to be, neither is getting the relevant permit. The locals are determined that there should be more integration in the community than before and are wanting to restrict the percentage of foreigners in the community to avoid getting swamped. Nevertheless, as long as you can fulfil the conditions of entry, and there is a place on the annual quota available, permits still can be obtained. **The first requirement is that you must own a property in Andorra.** No residence permit, as opposed to a work permit, now will be issued to a tenant. Conversely, owning or renting a property in Andorra does not oblige an owner to apply for a residence permit. PTs (officially) cannot stay for more than three months at a time. Pause for a minute. Think !! Do you really want a residence permit? First, foreigners in Andorra, given a very low profile, probably still can organize so that they use their Andorran address perpetually, Probably, no will bother you even if you are around on and off for years, provided you mind your own business and avoid making local enemies. Andorrans, as we have said, basically are anarchists. They dislike all governments. Even govrnment employees tend to think the same way. If you do not provide them with a big enough excuse to ask questions, they won't. With a reported 12 million tourists a year, why should they hassle you for staying too long. Anyway, there is nothing to stop you taking a short holiday away. In Switzerland, England or almost anywhere else, a low-profile person rarely will be challenged or have to face the demand: "Show me your papers."

Even though the Andorran government computer is probably not the worst computer to be in, staying out of all information banks should be your objective. So why register anywhere as a resident? Be a PT! If you do not know what a PT is, see the back of this report for a summary of Scope's best reports, *PT 1* and *PT 2*.

If you insist, application for residence must be made through the new office called *Oficina d'Estrangers* once you are settled. When making this application you will be asked to submit your passport and – if you are hitched – marriage certificate. You will need a reference or a certificate of good conduct from your last place of residence. A certificate of good conduct (no criminal record) is not a "must have", we are told, and British subjects who cannot get one anyway are normally passed through with a glowing reference from a professional person. But there are two further requirements, a health insurance cover note from a local company and plenty of money to support yourself. There is no doubt that future selection of new residents is going to be on the basis of how much of their assets they are prepared to commit to Andorra. We are also told that a diploma from a Catalan language course would be very impressive as showing willingness to "integrate". The one person they do not want is the person who actually admits that the only reason he wants to come is to avoid his obligations in his own country. Details of your (declared available) assets will go no further than the Immigration Office but it had better look pretty good for you to stand a chance. A small studio apartment is not going to impress!

There are new costs involved too. A payment for "social services" and a fairly large annual residence permit fee. If you wish to bring children in, to be educated in the free schools, there will be a charge for that and, if you do, you will be well down the list right from the start.

The application process, all in Catalan, has been made more complicated. You definitely will need the persuasive charms of a Service company or a local to help you along.

The decision to grant or withhold the new permit, or its renewal, will be made by the Andorran government, which, no doubt, in turn will continue to consult a special panel of your neighbors – on a very informal basis – as to your suitability, in the time-honored way of Andorra. This sort of thing is not uncommon in places where a large government bureaucracy does not exist.

If you wish to have a residence permit you must reside in the country for more than six months a year, otherwise you will lose your permit, except in rare cases where your "residence" will reflect well on Andorra. If you are Frederick Forsysth or Martina Navratilova you probably would be through in a flash, if you are Joe Nobody, join the queue!

A residence prmit does not entitle you to work in Andorra, not even in your "own" company. You can, of course, be a consultant outside Andorra and attract your worldwide income to Andorra. But if you wish to work, there are now lots of obstacles in your way, including having to go back out of the country to find your way to one of the new overseas "Pre-Selection" offices to be opened by the government. There, you will have to prove that your prospective employer – you cannot come as a self-employed person – has consulted the government as to your suitability and has a certificate proving that you are not taking a job away from a local. In principle, in future, the only way you are going to be able to prove that, unless you are something unusual like a cyberspace engineer and Andorra happens to be screaming for one, is to start your own company. Or rather, a company "run" by your Andorran sponsor, where you (officially, *see next section*) have a minority shareholding and the proposed business itself will not upset the local traders in the same line of work. If you are seeking work in one of the liberal professions, forget it, unless you happen to be the world's leading authority on your speciality AND you can speak perfect Catalan.

If you have the assistance of someone who really knows the ropes, you probably will get your work permit but be warned: you cannot bring your family into Andorra to live before you have worked for three years and even that privilege is controlled by quota. Dope

dealers, illicit share pushers, international swindler types and professional conmen are not welcomed in Andorra. But they probably wouldn't apply for a work permit anyway...

WHY IS ANDORRA NOT A BASE FOR OFFSHORE CORPORATIONS?

Why indeed? Because Andorra does not want them. Period! This country, without direct taxes, is already making more money than it can spend. We discovered that a good chunk of revenue is raised by "blackmailing" the major tobacco companies.

The scheme goes like this:

Every year, millions of visitor-smugglers, mostly from neighboring Spain, to a lesser extent from France, enter Andorra. Most of them are wholesale dealers from Barcelona or Toulouse. They stock up heavily on duty-free, tax-free, VAT-free cigarettes to such an extent that tiny Andorra has become a major market for the world's cigarette producers.

One of the few export products grown or produced in Andorra is tobacco. Andorran tobacco, however, is of inferior quality yet priced nine or ten times higher than going rates on the world market. You would think that there would be no buyers. Right? Wrong!

Actually, the majors are lining up to get their hands on Andorran tobacco. Each truckload purchased and exported entitles cigarette producers to a similar weight truckload import of the finished product: Marlboro, Pall Mall, etc.

Once the Andorran tobacco is sold, it is destroyed! All Philip Morris and the rest of the producers really care about is getting their share of the lucrative Andorran market for cigarettes. This they cannot get without purchasing almost all the tobacco Andorra itself produces. If you want to buy foul-smelling Andorran stogies, you can get them only in Andorra, some locals like them!

Naturally, this has led to Andorran tobacco farmers churning out tons of inferior quality hay. Rumor has it that this tobacco is wrapped around rocks to increase the weight of the bales sold.

These farmers can sit on their bums most of the time and do nothing else but make rock-rolled cigars. But as most of the tobacco produced belongs to the state under a co-op agreement, producing tobacco for destruction is a major source of national revenue. And with this set up, everybody's happy.

Taxes on the locals are thus avoided. With a small duty on other items bought by day tourists, other taxes are not needed to make the budget balance.

The Andorran model shows that with a sense of free market enterprise, Uncle Scrooge spirit and a dose of screwiness, anarchy, capitalism and blackmail can be used to benefit everyone.

A flat fee is levied on limited companies of 50,000 pesetas annually and 75,000 pesetas on a *Societat Anónima.*

Why doesn't Andorra cash in on the opportunity to become an "offshore corporation centre" catering to the tax-avoiders?

In the words of Candid Naudi i Mora, a member of one of the small number of families that dominate Andorra:

"We've seen what the nouveau riche money men have done in other so-called tax havens. The Arabs and the Asians have offered us blank cheques to set up their financial institutions here. We've politely told them that with a per capita income greater than that of the UK or USA, we do not want nor need their money". What's the result of this desire on the part of Andorrans to retain control of their own destiny? All legal entities (corporations) must be at least two-thirds owned by Andorrans. This insistence on strictly local control makes it difficult to conceive of Andorra as an international business base.

There is, however, a new willingness to open up the commercial sector to establish Andorra as an "offshore center". It is likely that the bank cartel soon will be broken and that new finance, bank and service companies will be allowed in a controlled manner. This will be a limited experiment to begin with but anybody with a good idea for a business which will assist Andorra to grow in a way that is wanted probably will find Andorra an ideal place. As always before, the person who digs his heels in, makes all the right moves, has plenty of finance and shows a willingness to integrate, probably will manage to prosper in Andorra.

WHY YOU SHOULD NOT FORM AN ANDORRAN CORPORATION

Contrary to popular belief, the Andorran Limited Company DOES exist. After a twilight period of several years, starting in 1973, it now is possible (only with two-thirds owned by local partners) to incorporate a business entity, which must have a minimum £15,000 paid up share capital. Naturally, there are no taxes on the income or capital gains earned by such an entity. There is not even a fixed annual duty or flat fee as in all other tax havens. Nor does a tax on earnings or dividends distributed exist. There is no requirement to file accounts with any authority. Andorra appears to be the tax haven to end all "corporate" tax havens. Unfortunately, it is largely reserved for Andorrans, non-Andorrans may not, of record or beneficially, own more than one-third of the capital stock of an Andorran company. Attempts to defeat this restriction through the use of fictions, trusts or other legal constructions are common, but risky. The financial arrangements and articles of incorporation will be vetted by the government on a case-by-case basis. **All nominee arrangements have been deemed unlawful.** Worse news? The majority of the board of directors (minimum of three directors), including the chairman, must always be Andorran.

Up to a point, there are ways around such restrictions on corporate ownership. But the implications are dangerous. Your Andorran partners must have full control. Thus, they can kiss you goodbye at any time. Furthermore, the fees charged by the required Andorran participants tend to be dear even if they are compliant straw-men or nominees.

To complete the dismal picture, the Andorran Commerce Registry refuses to register non-Andorran (or other non-resident) companies. There is no way to set up a branch of a foreign company.

To recap. At first sight, an Andorran corporation seems quite attractive with no taxes, no VAT, no obligation on book-keeping, unlimited capital movements, bank accounts in any currency etc. and you can get rid of unwanted "partners" by signing a deed of retrocession in front of a notary. But upon investigation Andorra as a corporate tax haven turns out to be expensive, difficult to manage, and in a gray area legally. For most property deals or international trading this arrangement is commercially unattractive, unless you really have a minority interest with Andorran partners.

The whole of this complex and restrictive system is being overhauled and reconsidered now that Andorra has its constitution. Andorrans now are completely free to decide their future. Servissim's monthly newsletter will give all the details of any moves to open up as they they come to hand. It is likely that during 1993/4 there will be unexpected developments and these will be covered in future editions of *The Andorra Report.*

The refusal, yet, to register local branches of foreign companies leaves the **only practical use of Andorra in the international corporate tax planning field as a residence or domicile for an individual**. This individual, in actual control and/or management of a corporation based somewhere else can draw a princely salary and pay no taxes. Sark currently plays host to on-island resident directors of thousands of corporations. Similarly, nothing prevents Andorran residents, whether or not they are Andorran nationals, from forming, owning, controlling, managing or being otherwise involved with **foreign companies** so long as such companies are not trading with or having an office within Andorra. There are, to our knowledge, no formal restrictions whatever in the area of operating any business from one's home or apartment.

Unfortunately, again, there may be informal sanctions. The foreigner resident in Andorra would do well to tread very cautiously. Publicised (or simply visible) attempts to use Andorra as an international corporate base to deal commercially with France or Spain must be made with great caution. In the long term, only quiet, low profile, strictly legal, small-scale or invisible activities by foreigners in Andorra are likely to be tolerated. Negative international publicity would be enough reason for the local authorities to suggest that you depart immediately.

Recently a group of corporate share peddlers calling themselves "Medatlantic", who had previously worked a bucket shop out of Holland, lasted only two weeks before being asked to leave Andorra.

"We have no formal agreements with Interpol but we exchange information. If we don't like someone, we politely tell them that we do not want to see them in Andorra tomorrow", says Sr Naudi, whose family controls Cisa, the major Andorran property developer.

THE COSMOPOLITAN VILLAGES OF ANDORRA

The town and villages of Andorra are all very cosmopolitan, with large numbers of PTs living everywhere. Officially, only 45,000 people live in Andorra. It is estimated, however, that about 15,000 foreigners have never registered with local authorities, thus bringing the total number of inhabitants up to 60,000 people.

Of the total population of 19,000 in Andorra la Vella, the capital, some 13,500 are foreigners. Similarly in Escaldes, where 12,000 people live, 9,000 are foreigners. In the British expatriate hide-out of La Massana (population 3,000), only 574 are native Andorrans, the rest are foreigners. Ordino, a quaint village with a lovely atmosphere and many cultural activities, has 700 foreigners out of 1,000 total.

In almost all other towns and villages the foreigners outnumber Andorrans three to one. Figures are obtained from the Andorran Conselleria de Treball i Benestar Social, a sort of census bureau. It states that the **total number of government officials and people employed by the state is a mere 100 persons**. Translating into a percentage figure relative to the number of inhabitants, only 0.18 per cent are on the public teat. Compare this figure with most European countries or the USA. There, one third to one half the total population have become "essential" bureaucrats. We always used to say that 90 per cent of government employees could be fired immediately without any noticeable difference, except for a major improvement in quality of life. Based upon the Andorra experience, it appears that 99 per cent of all bureaucrats could and should be urged to find more honest work.

HOW TO GET ANDORRA TRAVEL DOCUMENTS

In most small countries, favors – like getting a residence permit – can be obtained on an informal basis.

You may, however, cut through the red tape with strong local sponsorship. A friend of ours got his Andorra residence and work permit the day he arrived. Please note, though, for such treatment you would have to be on good terms with a local politician. Without a personal connection you would probably have to contribute something valuable to the community. It would be cheaper to use the services of Servissim.

In Andorra, getting a passport is something reserved for Andorrans. Yes, Andorra DOES issue its own passports. No, one does not easily become an Andorran. Immigration and naturalization is not a concept within their mentality. The only way of becoming Andorran, they will tell you, is by birth to two Andorran parents. Depending on to whom you speak in Andorra, opinions differ on this subject. The most often heard official explanation, however, is that if a child is born in Andorra to foreign parents residing full-time in Andorra, this child, if still resident at 18, can opt for Andorran citizenship.

Citizenship is granted immediately to women who marry an Andorran. It appears that a foreign girl marrying an Andorran male resident in Andorra automatically gains citizenship, thus becoming Andorran herself and eligible for an Andorran passport.

The scheme doesn't work for males unless the girl is the only daughter and last surviving member of an Andorran family. Then the guy can take over and perpetuate a family name that would otherwise have become extinct. Thus for stud service, you can become an "honorary native" Andorran entitled to a passport. We suspect also that with friends in the inner circles of the Andorra establishment anything is possible. Unfortunately, during our six weeks of on-site research, we weren't personally able to infiltrate the power elite as we did in Poland and Italy.

COMPARING GIBRALTAR AND ANDORRA

We prefer Andorra over Gibraltar as a place to live. We like the quiet, almost deserted valleys – the nature lover's ambience. The Andorran view of government is: "We ain't got many laws and we don't need any more". Others rave about Gibraltar. But the government there is decidedly socialist. If you are an old salt and not a ski-bum, Gibraltar might be more interesting to you for its port facilities and Med-Atlantic sailing opportunities. Andorra's weather is colder. Living way up in the mountains, you will get snowed in now and then during the winter.

Andorra is much less convenient to airports (Barcelona) and boat transport. No daily cheap flights to London as from the Rock of Gibraltar. But there are many ski charters from England where air passage, bus transfers, hotels and lift tickets come as a cheap package deal. Like Andorra, Gibraltar is also a cheap place for duty-free shopping and "everything" in consumer goods is available at discounts in both places.

Yet Gibraltar is urban, noisy and crowded. Its buildings are without much architectural merit. Cheap pubs, fish'n'chips and fast food joints are lined up one after the other. Its crowded, littered, Main Street is not the most charming in the world – especially when compared to the quaint and beautiful village squares of Andorra. Andorra's congested main drag running between France and Spain is just about as bad as Gibraltar's, but Gibraltar has no rural backwaters where one can escape and commune with nature. Andorra has thousands of acres with many secluded hilltop or valley farmhouses for sale or rent. As a peaceful, pleasant place to live, Andorra has much more to offer the discerning PT.

Gibraltar is unsuitable as a personal residence in our view. Even as a corporate tax haven there are some loose ends that worry us, only offshore-companies domiciled in Gibraltar may be sure of their no-tax status. Worst of all, the government is very leftist / socialist. We can never tell when (like Malta or Mexico's socialists have done several times), the present Gibraltar government just might seize everything. Then again, changing the rules ex post facto is not the British way of doing things... The British Laborites usually squeeze first, then confiscate through inflation, lethal taxes, levies and rates. But if they bleed you slowly or fast, the result is the same. The government gets all the chips and you lose them.

Gibraltar DOES have some uses, especially for the PT living in nearby Spain or Portugal. It's a good place for planting one of your asset management "flags". See the five-flag theory set forth in report *PT 1.* A Gibraltar corporation or trust is a good vehicle to use for non-Gibraltar businesses or real estate holdings. We wouldn't keep serious money in Gibraltar. Its only use in our view, is as a jurisdiction to form a corporate shell for legal tax avoidance.

Andorra, though we liked it **more** after a visit, is not 100 per cent Paradise on Earth either. To recap the drawbacks: it is not easy to get to. The nearest big Spanish town of Barcelona is at least a two and a half hour journey by car or bus. If you need an obscure part for your car or computer, you might not find it in Andorra. Gibraltar is more high-tech orientated. The main street through Andorra is often one 20-mile traffic jam. Local roads simply can't handle the excessive numbers of cars and busloads of tourists and shoppers. It is not practical to build a six-lane highway bypass through Andorra's mountains and valleys. The very LACK of massive central government, Andorra's most attractive feature, makes it unable to tackle mass transit or expensive problems of this nature. It is without resources for massive public works. On the plus side of the equation: Andorra is an absolutely "pure" tax haven with property prices and a cost of living far below that of Switzerland, Liechtenstein, Campione, Monaco or the Channel Islands.

Once you get off the congested and overbuilt main road, Andorra has many niches of great scenic beauty, clean mountain air, wild flowers, interesting birds. It teems with small wild animals. While not a sex-haven, it is an ideal hide-away to go with a lover for a few months. Andorra is a fine place to plant your residence flag, and an interesting country for real estate investments or banking. We rate it higher than Switzerland in both categories.

Verdict: Live part of the year in Andorra, buy property there if you like the place, open a bank account, consider making Andorra your fiscal center by using an address arranged by Servissim.

If you have an active business or need a property holding company, consider using Gibraltar's facilities for setting up a holding company or trust. But don't invest there. If you open a bank account in Gibraltar and use it as an asset base, deal only with a major international bank and get a written guarantee that your account is insured against all eventualities including government confiscation, by the parent bank. If they won't provide such a guarantee, deposit your money elsewhere.

The Andorra banks are exceptionally strong and any of them would be a good parking place for say, up to 25 per cent of your assets. [No matter how good something looks, it's always safer to diversify.]

OS & LLIVIA: THE SECRET ENCLAVES

If anyone looks at a good map of Andorra, it can be seen that there are many more routes in and out of Andorra than just the two manned border crossing points, one at Pas De La Casa (to France) and the other official border station near Saint Julia (to Spain). In fact there are at least a dozen other tracks suitable for four wheel drive vehicles. Still more paths to France or Spain are suitable only for hikers or pack animals. For the past 1,000 years, and until World War Two, one main occupation of Andorrans was smuggling contraband through the many unguarded mountain passes between France and Spain. There were no roads at all to Andorra until just before World War Two.

After this war, most Andorrans became far richer with less work by servicing tourists, building vacation homes for foreigners, and engaging in Swiss-style banking. However, it is still rumoured that for a reasonable fee certain families will pick up and deliver untaxed high value goods or undocumented people anywhere within Andorra, France or Spain. The philosophy of the native, old generation Andorra is very rugged individualist and "free market". We regret to note, however, that a new younger political group calling itself the Liberal Opposition (people who never had to struggle for a living) is doing a lot of talking about the need for increased government controls and being more like other modern countries. This new group already has pushed through building height limits, taxes on banks and local businesses, design controls, and more and more restrictions on foreigners.

With this historic background in mind, Gerhard Kurtz, the renowned German tax-haven author, recommends that freedom seekers who smell the beginning of the end in Andorra should immediately stake their claim to a bit of real estate in Os, a backwater Spanish town that can't be reached directly from Spain, but only via Andorra. [See our map]. As there are only a couple dozen properties in the entire town proper, we trust that all our readers won't go there at once. But if you do make inquiries or actually buy a place, please let the author know your experience – both as a matter of curiosity and as possible information for our next edition!

To get to Os, or Os de Civis as it is also known, you take the road from Saint Julia through Aixovall and Bixessarri. Then follow your nose and keep going. You can't go anywhere else! The road will probably be marked Carretera d'Os de Civis [road to Os]. After you have zigzagged until your steering arms are about to fall off, when it seems as though you have left the world behind you, you'll see a sign with the EC circle of yellow stars on a background of blue. "Welcome to Spain!" Nary a human being will be in sight. With luck, you may see some wild mountain goats called chamois or isard. These animals all stay on the Spanish side of the border due to being hunted to near extinction in Andorra. The road downhill will degenerate into a bumpy gravel track for another kilometre or so. The entire distance from the Andorra main highway is only about 10 km as the crow flies but the meandering, switchback road will seem more like 50 km. You follow a mountain stream known as Riu d'Os, pass lots of waterfalls, and climb through some spectacular mountain scenery. Bring a picnic lunch. Near the border, in the middle of nowhere, you'll come upon a pretty meadow. Sturdy tables and metal barbecue stoves will provide the setting for a feast of potato salad and hamburgers. Nobody is selling them – you must bring your own!

In about 40 minutes (from St Julia) you'll arrive in an old stone-built timeless Catalonian town. We are told that Os is like Andorra 50 years ago – before prosperity with a capital PT came to Andorra. That's a polite way of saying that Os looks more like a romantic ruin than anything else.

Journalist Kurtz writes about Os in his new book, *218 Tax Havens*. which can be ordered from Scope International Ltd, for US $150 post free. We always appreciate such information and are happy to give Kurtz a complimentary copy of the *Andorra Report* – just as we will do the same for any reader who furnishes other ideas or information we use.

THE OS OPPORTUNITY

There are no border formalities between Os and Andorra. There are no Spanish civil servants (nor police officers) in Os. No one could even tell you exactly where the border is, aside from the one place on the road where there's a sign. Well, perhaps the mountain goats know the border! This lack of definitions applies to much of the Andorran boundaries. No one cares about marking or fencing exact lines because the disputed (or should we say indefinite) areas are uninhabitable mountain ridges and shifting streams. But the fact is that **Os, Spain, cannot be reached with a normal car or truck by any land route from Spain**. The only access is via Andorra.

We drove into Os from Andorra with a big American (two wheel drive) station wagon in late 1992 and then tried to continue on into Spain. Five hundred metres out of Os we had to turn back due to the steepness of the grade and rocky terrain. It looked like we could have made it with a Jeep or Land Rover. This lack of connecting road to anywhere else in Spain is why Os could be of interest.

Kurtz tells this story: "Once upon a time, many years ago, the moment a Spanish tax collector pulled into town, a secret signal went out to all the villagers of Os. The tax collector knocked on doors. No one was at home. It seemed that the Earth swallowed up his 'clients.' The only people he found were a few 'Andorran visitors' who spoke no Spanish, refused to identify themselves, or even admit that the place was indeed Os. After several attempts to create a tax roster, the Spanish Hacienda (or tax collection agency) gave up and never tried again. They couldn't get the name of even one resident."

During our recent visit we saw a mail box in Os but no post office. There is no official mail delivery. Of course mail for the town does come into Os. It is regularly picked up in Andorra by the residents. There are no police in Os, nor do any Spanish government employees of any description ever seem to come visiting. The Mayor of the commune can be contacted through a guy who runs the bodega and general store that serves as the nucleus of downtown Os. It is the only store in town. By the way, lunch at this No Name Bar in Os is cheap and rustic – about what you'd expect in a Spanish town of under two dozen souls. There is a rumour that smuggling cigarettes and other items into Spain is still the major source of income here. We saw absolutely no visible economic activity. Nobody seems to farm or raise chickens. Outside of some impressive looking four wheel drive vehicles, there are no other signs of prosperity. Is there more in Os than meets the eye?

Our local guide to Os indicated that appearances could be deceiving. A Gothic-looking old farmer in well-patched pants (our guide said) just might have many, many kilos in gold coins squirreled away, buried in the mountains. The same country-hick sort of guy might share a hovel in the hills with several relatives and some sheep – without electricity, gas or even running water. Our guide, a new generation hotshot Andorran real estate broker with a Porsche, said that many people who looked and dressed like poor slobs were multi-millionaires with 30 generations of smuggling profits buried in the hills and very substantial bank accounts as well.

The same was true of the Os people, he said. They may look like jerks but if you shook hands in a business deal with them, you'd have no fingers left.

Apart from the jumble of pueblo style houses, all the land in the area is owned communally. It can be farmed or developed (by local custom), only with the unanimous permission of the entire commune. Foreigners are said to be welcome to settle in the community but the only newcomers in the last 1,000 years were a few couples from Barcelona who recently bought vacant, tumbledown buildings for a song and remodelled them nicely as summer homes. Reportedly, some are not used. It's said they may be for sale at 70 per cent below prices on similar properties within Andorra. The locals speak "only Catalan" but will possibly respond to your Spanish if sure you're not a cop, nark nor tax collector. As in Andorra, there are three types of property:

La Pleta – sort of a pueblo or shared wall development that is common in all the medieval towns of Europe. It differs from a modern condo apartment only in that it encompasses the whole town and rambles in every direction to fill up all liveable space within the fortified walls (which may or may not still exist). In most towns, many of these units are abandoned – but someone owns them, and the locals know exactly who owns what. As mentioned, we found these units to be too claustrophobic for our taste. Some modern buyers combine several units on several floors and create an attractive, good sized apartment. As ground floors were often used to house animals in winter, there is usually ample garage and storage space.

Then there is the Xalet or Chalet – a single family home on its own lot. These days they must be built of local stone to blend in with existing properties.

Bordas or stone barns are found in many design variations all over the hills. Formerly used for animals or storing and processing agricultural products, property in the borda category is the most desirable and sought after. A borda is always a very big structure with many unique touches. If imaginatively remodelled it can offer magnificent interior space and character by retaining old stone ovens, fireplaces, and animal feeding troughs. These may be made of hand-hewn oak or hand-chipped stone. Apertures can become picture windows or sites for stained-glass art work. A borda could be the equivalent of three or four stories high.

Cheap electricity comes in from Andorra. There are no phones. A cellular phone can be used with connections via a central station in Andorra. No one has done it yet. But then appearances could be deceptive. Satellite dishes for TV were not in evidence but if one were installed the whole town should be able to receive dozens of stations including CNN (news in English) and Sky channel (sports and films in English) as they do in Andorra.

WHY CONSIDER OS?

For the tax-exile, **it is much easier to get a Spanish resident's permit in Os**than in Andorra. In Andorra, these days you practically have to buy a property to be granted a resident's permit. The cheapest homes in Andorra cost around £150,000. Even the worst, grotty Andorra apartment would be around £30,000. But residence in Spain (where property is cheap) is automatic if one is already a citizen of the EC. You don't have to buy either. Simply **rent an apartment** or a caravan (house-trailer) space.

An apartment in Os, if one could be found, might be as cheap as £1,000. That is to **buy it**, not rent it for a month! Of course in this price range any such "apartment" would be walls and a pile of stones, La Pleta style. Still, wouldn't £1,000 plus another £10,000 to create a liveable space be a cheap price to pay for avoiding income tax and confiscatory inheritance taxes?

A Swede, Dane or German cannot escape his own country's taxes unless he moves **not** to a tax haven, like Andorra but to a place with a similarly confiscatory tax system. There is not much point in moving out of the frying pan and into the fire by signing on for unknown obligations as bad as the ones you are trying to escape. Of course once the home country is convinced you really live in Spain, after a year or two you can move anywhere and be a PT. Os de Civis, Kurtz says, offers the perfect solution. It's easy to get a resident visa for Spain. Even without such a visa, you need no permission to rent, buy or otherwise settle in Os. Os is unquestionably Spanish. The Mayor of Os might even be willing to rent you a room in his cellar or attic as your address of convenience. We have not made any such arrangement with him but the odds are an understanding can be worked out for a price similar to the £550 per year deal with Servissim in Andorra. But you'd have to go there personally. Then, once legally resident in Spain, like all the other residents of Os (and Andorra), you simply don't pay taxes. No one cares what you do or where you go.

IS OS THE PERFECT SOLUTION?

Zsa Zsa Gabor, when asked "Would you sleep with a perfect stranger?" reportedly replied, "Nobody is perfect!" Likewise, no place is perfect either. This author's observation is that if you really like Os, then go for it. Maybe even buy a place there and live happily ever after – on $2 bathtub gin and half-price cigarettes. But if you hate the place, look for other solutions as described in *PT 1.* Man does not live by tax avoidance alone. And as we will mention later, in our opinion, the tax haven status of Os probably wouldn't survive any real influx of free spending tax-exiles with serious money to shelter.

BANISHED FROM ANDORRA'S TAX PARADISE? STAY IN THE GARDEN OF EDEN BY MOVING TO OS!

Another aspect of Os is that in accordance with long established usage and ancient treaties, Andorra may not deny the use of its public roads to anyone wishing ingress or egress to Os. Kurtz says this could have interesting implications for the many individuals who have been banished from Andorra. True or false? Could people banished from Andorra move to Os and keep doing whatever got them banished? The author feels that Andorra's police could get rather rough on, say, felons or convicted drunk drivers who were banned from Andorra, "moved" to Os, and then still insisted upon their **rights** to spend time in Andorra.

THE WIZARD OF OS

We feel that after being declared *persona non grata* in Andorra it is a good idea to avoid further confrontations. Andorran police are well known for leaving people alone but also for dealing rather roughly with unwelcome foreigners who abuse local hospitality. There are no American-style "Constitutional Rights" in Andorra. Police brutality and Wild West style justice are still in fashion there. For those who are kicked out of Andorra for misconduct and manage to survive the "tar and feathering" ceremonies in one piece, it is, in our view, extremely unlikely that Spain would stand up for the rights of a black sheep, just because he claimed to be living in Os.

Sure, a low profile guy could go back and forth into Andorra from Os all he wanted to. But the Andorrans could and would clap someone they considered an undesirable into their dungeons – or worse, for violating an order to get out (and stay out) of town. And unless some criminal mastermind made them an offer they couldn't refuse, the villains of Os probably wouldn't want another brigand in their town. So unless you have the financial resources and political skills to win the whole town over, and cut them all in on your schemes, don't expect to be able to run any international smuggling operations from Os. They don't want any foreigners muscling in to become the Wizard of Os.

BARGAINS ON HOUSES IN OS

Real estate prices in Andorra (though cheap in comparison to other tax havens) are certainly ten times the prices of land and unremodelled buildings in rural towns like Os just across the border in Spain or France. It is theoretically possible that someone who loved the Andorra lifestyle and wanted to buy in cheaply could make a good deal in Os. Then as we said, one could shop daily and buy cheap booze and cigarettes in Andorra, and live happily ever after. Of course it should be remembered that the connecting houses of picturesque little Os are now a "classified structure". Os has a building code protecting the exterior of all old structures from any changes. This law is similar to Andorra's. This means that hand cut stone building exteriors can't be fundamentally changed, they must be restored. It is also said to be nearly impossible for a newcomer to get permission to build a new house. But clearly, if one ingratiated oneself with the locals, almost anything is possible, same as in Andorra!

In Os, most of the original interior rooms are small, gloomy, cold, damp, and with tiny windows. As the massive stone walls are all bearing walls, they can't be moved or eliminated except at great expense. This author wouldn't like to live in such cramped quarters with neighbors on all sides. Some might find the atmosphere and tiny winding streets claustrophobic. There are however, a few abandoned stone barns in the hills that might be picked up for the price of a dinner for two at Tour D'Argent in Paris. Similar barns in Andorra have been done up as very comfortable, sturdy homes, matching in basic design the Park Hotel. Rarely on the market, these huge old Andorra barns are much desired by wealthy expats when converted and conversions sell for £300,000 and more. If you wanted to do it yourself over a long period, or find a way (helicopter?) to bring in remodelling materials, generators, and a crew of fast workers, converting a Spanish barn near Os could be an option. Because of the inaccessibility, the eventual cost, even without the extra expense of installing a road, might be as much as a ready-built place on a maintained road in Andorra. Still, if you wanted to be a hermit...

REAL-LIFE REVELATION – REHABILITATING A RUIN

One handy friend and client actually bought such a remote ruin in a different country, South America, not Europe. We thought he was nuts as there were just four walls and a leaky roof to start with. No running water, no electricity, no phone and no road. Worst of all, there was no prospect that there would ever be any such municipal services. But our guy personally rigged up a turbine generator in a local mountain stream for unlimited free power. He installed a radio-phone and solar panels for back-up power, he ran pipes to a modern bathroom and kitchen. Finally he graded a nearby meadow for his own private airstrip. For the price of a nice suburban home, he has a rather splendid and spacious private domain that is isolated, yet self-sufficient. He finished the project just before the USSR fell apart. One reason for it was to have a personal haven for surviving the nuclear holocaust he felt was at hand. With this reason evaporated, he still likes his hideaway but as he seldom uses it, he is ready to sell at a loss. At least his place could be reached by private plane as well as four-wheel drive vehicles. Not so in Os.

The lack of any level land prevents the landing of fixed wing aircraft in Andorra or Os. You could commute by helicopter, and two or three Andorran people own helicopters. But at £75,000 minimum for a used chopper, and a big investment in learning how to fly it, most people have to get to civilization with only their Jeeps. In the winter they will often be snowbound. When the snow melts, they'll still need an hour of driving time to get into town.

Like owners of private islands, you have to be a very special person to want to start such a major project and end up with such isolation. Will your spouse, girlfriend or kids like the place? Would you like it if no one wants to be your playmate up there with the mountain goats? Can you find happiness without the ability to get in your car and drive to a nearby grocery for a dozen eggs or a few cans of beer? A degree of self-sufficiency is nice but most of us prefer to have the benefits of civilization more conveniently at hand, without the disadvantages of bad or no roads. Even if you are very rich, as a few of our clients are, and even if you can afford a helicopter or yacht and servants to run and fetch things, most of us prefer to avoid dependence on other people or machinery. Besides, if you need servants, where's the benefit of your seclusion? Sometimes servants quit, leaving you in the lurch. Sometimes helicopters don't work or are quarantined by weather. Aircraft, especially helicopters, are inherently more dangerous than cars. For those who live on private islands, boats are just as bad, they often founder when caught in unexpected squalls or ice. The fact is that most people who buy or build island or mountain retreats are fulfilling a fantasy. After a short period, be it months or a year, they get tired of it. Then again, our PT readers are individualists, **unlike** most other people. Some of us may thrive in seclusion. How about you?

WOULD OS BE A HAVEN FOR A HIGH PROFILE OR ACTIVE DRUG DEALER?

Probably not. Everywhere and anywhere is a good hideout for a person with a shady past provided he keeps a low profile, has good papers and is perceived as a tourist who doesn't stay more than about six months at a time. It is always easier to be anonymous in a bustling transient resort or a big city! Os would be as good a place as any small town. But small towns are not so good for persons who want to be anonymous. To interdict a major criminal, the Spanish government could and certainly would send in helicopters or attack team of Land Rovers without crossing into Andorra. And the Andorrans would hardly object to an internationally known foreign bad guy being forcibly evacuated from Os, whether through Andorra or not. Os and Andorra protect their own bad guys, some of whom are pillars of the community – but foreigners are expendable. Fugitive or not, certainly doing a major rehab on a substantial dwelling in Os could bring unwelcome bureau-rat attention. The good people of Os have been low profile for centuries. They would probably resent a newcomer who didn't try to blend in and assimilate. The reason the Spanish tax collector hasn't come to Os in force is that right now there is apparently nothing worth going after. The family of Pedro de Poverti and his neighbors if pressed would probably ask for and get more in welfare benefits than they would pay in taxes. Those Barcelona proprietors of vacation places in Os are already in the Spanish tax net and would not be a source of new income tax receipts. You might be! We personally would not bet our ass and assets on Os. A small apartment would probably escape attention. Not the same for a visible major deluxe home. Better to be a low profile PT in Barcelona or any big city. You could rent a palace in any resort or big town for six months and the tax guys wouldn't bother you. But forgetting all other considerations, would Os suit you? That's the real question. Our needs and desires are all different. Just because this author would rather be in Monaco doesn't mean you feel the same way. Os does have its uses – if you like the place and use it correctly. It wouldn't be a bad place to own a small apartment. It could be a mail drop that you call "home" but seldom visit. Or you could stay there during the several months (May through October) when you wouldn't be snowbound.

For an English or American guy wishing to avoid a jail sentence for not paying alimony, taxes or parking tickets in his home country, it is hardly likely that the Spanish would co-operate in any extradition from Os. But then the same thing would be true in Paris, Milan, Madrid or Barcelona where one could live far more anonymously. It is always easier to get lost or take on a new identity in a city. In Os as in every little town, anything to be known about a new foreigner in town would be prised out or discovered in due course. And with the usual tendency of small town people to snoop, gossip and magnify, it is extremely difficult to have any privacy. What if a spouse, your kids or other indiscreet visitors come to see you? Scenario, they are questioned by the neighbors. Soon the whole town knows your secrets. On the other hand, the right person could win over the locals, with a local marriage-alliance perhaps?, and gain some in-depth protection.

ARE YOU LIKELY TO MAKE A KILLING ON OS PROPERTY?

Find out if the Barcelona folks will be pulling in a bundle of fat profits if and when they sell? I doubt it. The theoretical market value of a nicely remodelled three-bedroom apartment in Os would be around £35,000. Sure, a three-bedroom view apartment in Monaco just sold for £2,000,000. But Os isn't Monaco and never will be. Rich people spend lots of money to live near other rich people. Places with snob appeal have built up a reputation over many years. Sometimes, a developer like Donald Trump in New York can give his particular project amenities resulting in a cachet or snob appeal greater than in a similar building next door. This was done in Porto Banus, Spain, by dredging out yacht berths for all the residents of this subdivision on the Mediterranean Sea. It's a few hundred miles south west of Os. At Porto Banus you get fashionable restaurants, discos, major supermarkets, airport, trains and bus services. Plus all the comforts of a major holiday destination. And at currently depressed prices in the Spanish tourist belt (1994) you'll get a pretty fair three-bedroom, sea view apartment for £40,000. This is only slightly more than you'd pay in Os for similar facilities. Porto Banus is not a tax haven of course but if you wanted a place to stay under six months a year, there would be no tax problems and Porto B would offer many more diversions than Os. If a PT spends under six months a year in a high-tax country and then leaves, he has the same no-tax situation as spending all his time in a tax haven. Thus, why buy property at an inflated price in a tax haven? You can live like a potentate in places like Kuaii, Morea, and Phuket. You'd not be bothered for taxes as a tourist and you'd spend only a tiny fraction of the income earned on money you didn't put into property! In our view, the only reason to buy property in a tax haven is if you insist upon staying in one place all the time and maintaining a high profile and engaging in conspicuous consumption. This attitude is of itself a big mistake, we feel. Why? Because even in a tax haven the rules could change if the local majority felt they could gain by confiscating the property of richer neighbors.

Young men, especially, want to make a big splash. They say to the world, "Hey look at **Me**!", regardless of consequences. Thus, we feel if you must make a statement, it is better to rent big showy places while on trips. Own (if you must) a disposable, cheaper place as your home base. We also advise make the choice of where you live based upon what you like, not just the tax haven status of the place. In fact, once you get off the tax rolls, as a PT, you can live anywhere you want, as long as you want. Within reason, and with care, you can be as high profile as you want. The secrets of how to pull this off are found in our other reports, *PT 1* and *PT 2*. Basically, if you are a visitor to a place, you can be outrageous without consequences. Where you live, be more circumspect. The underworld proverb is "Don't defecate where you eat".

Returning to the question, **will there be a real estate boom in Os**? Answer: maybe. If some developer comes in, gets the Spanish tax laws changed to create a "free port" and does a major rehab and advertising blitz. To get prices like Monaco's, besides tax freedom, Os might need an opera house, a live-in prince, museums, art galleries, live theatre, several casinos, 20,000 rich and famous residents, a very salubrious year-round climate – and for good measure, perhaps a marina on the Mediterranean Sea. Not very likely for an inaccessible little town of 24 permanent residents. But then, New York City was inaccessible once. Given imagination and enough money, maybe Os will become another Monaco. But without a major change in Spanish laws, it isn't likely.

WOULD YOU BE JUSTIFIED IN PAYING A PREMIUM FOR PROPERTY IN THE 'TAX HAVEN' OF OS DE CIVIS?

In our opinion, even **one** substantial investment in a house by a very rich foreigner would bring the tax snoopers back to Os. If you weren't home, the Hacienda could cause a tax assessment to be nailed to the door. Then, in due course, if you didn't file tax returns or contest the assessments, your property could be confiscated and sold for taxes. You'd be required to have a universal tax and ID number issued by Spain. **The tax haven feature of Os is not protected by law**, nor is it even likely to exist if any high-profile wealthy individual moved there. One could get a better tax deal in sunny Italy, Costa Rica, or many other places where all foreigners without local source income are not harassed by the local tax leeches – at least for the time being. Spain, with the USA, Japan, Germany and the Scandinavian countries, has the most grasping and all-powerful tax collection system on Earth. The new policy in Spain is squeeze the foreigners till their pips squeak. Property owners in Spain are taxed on their worldwide income unless they can prove they are paying taxes in another country and protected by treaty. This new policy in Spain is why foreigners in Spanish resort cities are moving out in droves and selling their secondary residences to Spaniards at one-third of what they were worth five years ago. It is the reason why you can pick up a bargain in Porto Banus. And the big bad Spanish Hacienda is why many former British retirees in Spain, and many Spaniards as well, have been buying in Andorra and establishing residences there. Many people believe that to avoid heavy taxes it is necessary to actually live physically in a tax haven. In *PT 1*, we showed that this is a myth. The only thing one needs to do is to move assets and body physically – to practically anywhere else in the world but the place where you are now paying taxes. Actually living in a tax haven is to be considered by the rational human being only if he wants to actively and openly run a major international business operation or professional practice with fixed assets and a highly visible income. Barring this circumstance, there are better ways to eliminate taxes.

Finally, unless one likes to be in a tiny mountain village, there are more pleasant places to live, and other places with more reliable communications than in Os. It is cold and damp, especially in the winter, because the town receives little sun for about nine months. This is due to its unfortunate positioning in the shade of the mountains. Needless to say, outside of visiting the one bar and general store with its postcards, rough red wine and rustic, mountain dried meats, there isn't a lot to do in Os. You can watch the wind blow or take hikes in the mountains. If you like Alpine climate, peace and quiet, maybe Os is your cup of tea. In summary,

Os got me all excited.
It was nice to be invited.
Though nice for a day;
I wouldn't want to stay!
But visit I plead
It could fill **your** need

And if it does, also have a look at the other secret enclave, a fiscal paradise we discovered East of Eden...

IF YOU'RE DINGY OVER OS, YOU'LL LOVE LLIVIA!

For another unusual geographic experience, on the east side of Andorra one can visit another Spanish enclave: **LLIVIA.** Similar to Os, this forgotten backwater is entirely surrounded by **France**. The Spanish Hacienda isn't active there either. Llivia, a town that's seen better days, is in a state of quiet decay, forgotten by all, and about 40 km by road across the French border, just below the Puigcerda boundary crossing. Real estate is as cheap as anywhere in France or Spain and that's really cheap. The town isn't anything to write home about. Maybe you can figure out some way a PT could use a Spanish enclave, of Catalan affinity, accidentally in France to advantage. If so, let me know.

Most of what we said about Os de Civis also applies to Llivia. So don't suggest that it would be a fine base for smuggling. We can figure that possibility out for ourselves. It may, like Os, be a good stopping-off point for EC citizens prohibited from moving directly to a blacklisted tax haven. No question that it has a better road to it than Os does. Also, you can be in a major city in France in less than one hour instead of about three from Os. If you come up with a new angle and want to do a Special Report on Llivia and/or Os, let us know! The restaurant in Llo, France, that we recommended as a stop before Andorra is very near Llivia. Any reader reports on places to stay or eat in Llivia, or more information "fit to print" on Os will be published in our next revision. Contributors get a free book!

OS AND LLIVIA COMPARED WITH CAMPIONE

For those who ask why we favor Campione (an Italian enclave in Switzerland) over these two Spanish enclaves, the answer is:

1. Italy does not tax foreigners without a local income. There are no ID or universal tax numbers. Spain, like France, goes after the world-wide income of foreign property owners living within its borders unless they can show they are really resident abroad more than six months per year and pay income taxes elsewhere. All **foreigners** who rent (long term) or own property, or have a phone or get electricity from the Spanish power company are required to have a tax ID number and file tax returns, with criminal penalties and massive fines if they don't. This doesn't apply to Os where there are no phones nor electricity from the Spanish government.
2. Campione residents have excellent communications – phone lines, postal services and banking services all provided by Switzerland. Os has notably bad communications. There is only one poor road for access.
3. Transport in and out of Campione is by convenient cheap vaporetto (boat) every ten minutes. The boats go to various points in Switzerland and Italy. Going to shop in Como via a picturesque boat is a pleasant experience that is more like the Grand Canal in Venice than the Coney Island Ferry. There is also a major intercity train service at Lugano, ten

minutes away. There are several major international airports in the vicinity. First class, all-weather super-highways connect Campione with all of Europe. You can commute to the major city of Milan in 40 minutes. Lugano and Chiasso, both major Swiss cities with perhaps 200 different banks to choose from, are minutes away.

4. Campione is a civilized place. A few secluded mountain hideaways – with a good road to them, are available at not too much more than Andorra prices. Ski-lifts are within convenient walking range as are beaches with swaying palm trees. The weather is better in Campione.

Os has none of the above amenities and, being part of tax-grasping Spain, owning property there could be like putting your head in a hungry lion's mouth... The tax collectors have ignored Os and Llivia till now but if they smelled big money, how long would it take for them to take a bite out of your hide?

ADVANTAGES OF OS AND LLIVIA?

In summary, for individuals prohibited by law or circumstances from moving directly to a tax haven, Os or Llivia could be worth considering. You could rent or buy a place for an intermediate stopping off place and to secure a legal residence. Then, when your home country deleted you from tax rolls, you could move on to happier hunting grounds – that is, unless you fell in love with the place. Thirty thousand other foreigners think that Andorra is the cat's meow. You might really enjoy yourself in Os or Llivia. Especially if you like mountain goats. Visit first. Let me know your reactions. Author's Note: The Harry Schultz of German Newsletter writers is Gerhard Kurtz who writes for *Geldbrief*, or *The Money Letter*, published by "Socrates" in Campione, Italy. He sent me the ideas and some of the information for this unique and imaginative contribution to our *Andorra Report*.

EPILOGUE

We will continue to look for places that are good or better than our present favorites:

1) Monaco for high profile, conspicuous consumption, and very fancy expensive females;

2) Campione for those who like the idea of living inside neutral Switzerland and who want to get an Italian passport free after seven years;

3) Andorra becomes our top choice as a tax free, very inexpensive retirement hide-out.

Look for Hill Reports in the works. Do you have any suggestions for future Hill reports? Would you like to write one as my co-author? Let me know.

We as PTs should help each other and not be selfish [information] collectors and hoarders. If you discover some interesting or useful facts, please pass them on to Scope. Do you see anything in this report that should be corrected or updated? Please let me know!

RESOURCE LIST - ANDORRA

ADVERTISING MEDIUM:

There are no English language publications in Andorra, except Servissim's private newsletter. New publications include *Andorra Magazine, Actual*, and a daily paper *Diari d'Andorra*. However, throughout the publishing scene there is a strict all-Catalan rule. Advertisements rarely are accepted in any other language.

Radio Valira will accept advertising in English but only from 2.30 - 3pm during its English program. The listening audience is limited.

AMBULANCE SERVICE:

Dial 118 on the telephone and say "Emergència Medical". Give your address. First aid for ski accidents is said to be excellent with helicopter evacuation service capable of delivering an injured party to Toulouse or Barcelona for any service not available locally. Urgent medical services are available by dialling 16.

AMBULANCES

Ambulancies Creu Blava
Prada Guillamo, s/n
Tel: 20 8 01
Andorra La Vella

Ambulancia Taxi-Areny
Avda. d'Encamp, 15 1Edifici Gran Duc
Tel: 55 3 08
Pas De La Casa

Servei D' Ambulancies
"Urgencies"
Telefons: 16 - 18

Servei D'Ambulancies-Bombers
Avda. Riberaygua
Tel: 20 0 20
Andorra La Vella

APARTMENTS - SHORT TERM

Residence Cosmos, Av de les Escoles 10, Escaldes Engordany Tel: 37-8-77. Fax: 37-7-30.

La Pubilla, Crta de La Massana, Escaldes Tel: 20-9-81

ARMAMENTS:

Want to equip a small army? Machine guns, cannons, bazookas,Mig jets, tanks, USA and Soviet army uniforms, boots, mobile kitchens and field hospitals – all available at discount prices, over the counter from SUPERVENCIA MILITARY SURPLAS, Carrer Comte Pere d'Urgell, 11, Andorra La Vella. (PO Box 1094). Tel. 60-21-5 Fax: 26-38-3. Store located next to French Post Office at Pont (Bridge) Prat de la Creu.

ART GALLERIES:

Era Bauro, Antic Carrer Major, 30, And. La Vella. (Specialist in Picasso & Miro).

AUTOMOBILE DEALERS (NEW)

Automobils Pyrenees (part of the store group), La Margineda, Sant Julia. Tel:41935. BMW, Mercedes (the only such joint agency in the world), Suzuki and Rolls-Royce/Bentley

4 x 4 Tot Terreny, Avda. Enclar 108, Santa Coloma. Tel: 61817. All-terrain vehicles

Auto Servei, Av Princep Benlloch 3, Andorra la Vella. Tel: 20745. Ford

Sport, Verge de Pilar 12, Andorra la Vella. Tel: 20144. Nissan, Range Rover, Saab

Internacional, Av Tarragona 27, Andorra la Vella. Tel: 21492. Peugeot

Cosmos, Av Les Escoles 10, Escaldes. Tel: 21266. Mazda

Toyota Motors, Av Fiter i Rossell 4, Escaldes. Tel: 22371. Toyota, Subaru

Becier, Av Santa Coloma, Santa Coloma. Tel: 63555. Renault, Chrysler

Vda. Rossell, Av Meritxell 100, Andorra la Vella. Tel: 21374. Volkswagen, Audi

Motorauto, Av Santa Coloma 50. Tel: 20423. Opel, Isuzu, GM, GME

CIMEX, Av Dr Mitjavila 5, Andorra la Vella. Tel: 23190. Fiat

Europ Auto, Carrer Dr Vilanova 7, Andorra La Vella. Tel: 25671. Seat

Automobils Alfa-Romeo, Baixada del Moli, Andorra la Vella. Tel: 21632. Alfa-Romeo

Automobils Jordi, Av Santa Coloma 89, Andorra la Vella. Tel: 20383. Lancia

Auto-Diesel, Verge de Canolich, Sant Julia. Tel: 41143. Volvo

Garatge Central, Carretera General, Encamp. Tel: 32400. Jaguar, Citroen, Rover

AUTO & MOTORCYCLE PARTS & ACCESSORIES

Casa Del Pneumatic, Av Santa Colima 34, And. La Vella.

MotoSprint, Av Santa Coloma, 88, And. La Vella

Special section at the Pyrenees Dept. Store.

Font Del Ferro, Ave Verge de Canolich 130, St Julia

(customization & kits)

Goodyear Tyres (“Pneumatics” in Catalan), Av F. Cairat, Av S.

Coloma 32 or 104, And St Julia. La Vella.

BABY CLOTHES:

Bambini, C/Bonaventure Armengol, 5, And. La Vella.

Piccolino, Carrer Riberaygua, 38, And La Vella.

BANKING: SEE ALSO CHAPTER ON THIS SUBJECT

The Spanish-owned bank La Caixa, recommended for current accounts, has the following branches in Andorra

Andorra La Vella, Placa Rebes, 3

Encamp, Coprincep Episcopal, 6

Escaldes, Pare Enic Graner 3

La Massana, Carretera General, sin. - “Casa Gabriel”

St. Julia de Loria, Verge de Canolic 55 Avinguda

BOOK ON ANDORRA

[Highly Recommended]: Andorra the Unknown Tax Haven, by James Barrington. £60 by mail order from Servissim, Av Meritxell 20, Andorra La Vella or from the author at 4 Akehurst Lane, Sevenoaks, Kent, TN13 1JN UK.

BUS SERVICES

City Sprint in London has a round-trip service in the summer and winter ski season from London's Victoria Bus Terminal. The fare is about £80 round trip and the journey (each way) takes about 24 hours. Travel agents advertising package deals to Andorra in the London Sunday newspapers will also sell space on their chartered buses (or planes) without the rest of the package if you wish to make your own land arrangements. Buses (called coaches or Pullmans in Europe) connect with the nearest train stations at L'Hospitalet or Ax les Thermes in France. There are also bus connections to Andorra from most towns in Spain. A direct bus from Barcelona leaves from Ronda De La Universidad.

COMMUNICATIONS:

French Post Office (Correus francesos)	20408
Spanish Post Office (Correus espanyols)	20257
Directory enquiries (Informacio telefonica)	11
Radio Nacional	63777
Radio Valira	29600
Communications Service (Servei de Communications)	21021

DEPARTMENT STORES & HYPERMARKETS

See chapter on Shopping for recommendations

ESTATE AGENTS/PROPERTY & RENTAL BROKERS

AGENCE LE GRIFFON, Av d'Encamp, Tel: 55008-55169-55216-55250, PAS DE LA CASA

ARIES, Ed. la Solana, local 2, Tel: 36432/36428, LA MASSANA

AUDIGESTIO, Av Riberaygua, Ed. Jupiter, Tel: 25490, ANDORRA LA VELLA

BENET, Av Fiter i Rossell, 74, Tel: 27097, ESCALDES

BUSCAT, Av Co-Princep FrancVs, Tel: 31060, ENCAMP

CAMP DEL SOL, Ed. La Solana, Tel: 31974, ENCAMP

CISA (Andorra), CONSTRUCCIO IMMOBILIARIA S.A., Edifici La Cabanota, La Massana, Tel: 35228/35055, Fax: 35035, ANDORRACOMANDOR, Av Co-Princep FrancVs, Tel: 31786, ENCAMP

EIOP, Placa Sant Jordi, s/n, Tel: 21140-24015, ESCALDES

ES PAI EQUIP S/S, Crta General-Casa Rossell, Tel: 36889, LA MASSANA

EURO 3, C. Joan Maragall, s/n, Tel: 26925, ANDORRA LA VELLA

FINANDOR ACG., Av Princep Benlloch, 8, Tel: 21806, ANDORRA LA VELLA

FINQUES CABRE, Dr. Nequi, 8, Tel: 26313, ANDORRA LA VELLA

FINQUES DEL PIRINEU, Av Meritxell, 67-desp. 101, Tel: 20554, ANDORRA LA VELLA

FONT, Av Carlemany, 55, Tel: 21340-23999, ESCALDES

GESTANDOR, C. Dr. Nequi, 7 3, Tel: 25252, ANDORRA LA VELLA

GESTIM, Av Riberaygua, 27, 1a pis., Tel: 23263-23465-28788, Fax: 25693 - Telex: GRUP 284 AND, ANDORRA LA VELLA

GISA, Crta. de la BordaTel: 21500-27500, ANDORRA LA VELLA

GRUPINSA, Dr. Vilanova, Ed. Davi, Of. 5o 2a, Tel: 24581 Fax: 61647, ANDORRA LA VELLA

HABITAT, Av d'Encamp, 2, Tel: 55074-55282, PAS DE LA CASA

IMMOBILIARIA D'ENCAMP, Crta. del Tremat, Ed. Telecadira, Tel: 31813-31232 Fax: 32590, ENCAMP

IMMOSERVEI "LA BORSA IMMOBILIARIA DEL PRINCIPAT", C. Ciutat de Valls, 20, Tel: 26770 Fax: 60206, PO Box 135, ANDORRA LA VELLA

IMMO TELE VIDEO, C/Ciutat de Valls, 20, Tel: 26770 Fax: 60244-60206, Mnt. 61186, ANDORRA LA VELLA

IMMOVACANCES, C. Major, Tel: 55004, PAS DE LA CASA

INVERLANE, Av Princep Benlloch, 56-3o, Tel: 29099, ANDORRA LA VELLA

INVERSIONS F ESPOT, 4th Floor, Avinguda Meritxell, 67, Tel: 22116, ANDORRA LA VELLA

INVICO, Av Meritxell, 20, Tel: 20019, Fax: 60537, ANDORRA LA VELLA

LAND SA, Av Meritxell, 99 1o 2b, Tel: 61820 Fax: 60407, ANDORRA LA VELLA

LES VALLS, Av Meritxell, 67, Tel: 24015, ANDORRA LA VELLA

MASSANDOR, Casa Gabriel baixos, Carrer General, Tel: 36481/36398, Fax: 37494, LA MASSANA

MORA, Av Princep de Gaulle, 13, Tel: 23979, ESCALDES

NEU I MAR, Av Meritxell, 85 2o, Tel: 25506, ANDORRA LA VELLA

NORMA, Av Princep Benlloch, 10, Tel: 23535-27749, ANDORRA LA VELLA

OFESIM, Gal. Paris, 3, Tel: 20344, ANDORRA LA VELLA

ORDINO, Casa Font, Tel: 36715-36202, ORDINO

PRIMEX, C. Isabelle Sandy, 6 1o 3a, Tel: 22902-24210, ESCALDES

PROMECSA, C. Fiter i Rossell, 1, Tel: 21118, ANDORRA LA VELLA

PROMOTORA NACIONAL, Av Carlemany, 109, Tel: 22409, ESCALDES

PROMOVALL, C. Ciutat de Valls, 26, Tel: 26852, ANDORRA LA VELLA

ROC PROPIETATS, Edifici Sant Roc, Planta Comercial, Carretera d'Ordino, Tel: 35346, Fax: 36674, LA MASSANA

ROSSELL, Av Riberaygua, 4, Tel: 25822, ANDORRA LA VELLA

SUPERIOR, C. de la UniX 2-2o, Tel: 21050, ANDORRA LA VELLA

TERRA NOSTRA II, C. Dr. Nequi, 9, Tel: 21644, ANDORRA LA VELLA

TREVOL, Placa Reves, 1, Tel: 2666, ANDORRA LA VELLA

URBANDOR, C. Isabelle Sandy, 3, Tel: 22202, ANDORRA LA VELLA

VICENT FINQUES, C. Babot Camp, 2, Tel: 21801-21829, ANDORRA LA VELLA

VILA SERVEI, C.Dr. Nequi, 7 Ed. Triangle 4 F, Tel: 26369 Telex: 336 VILASERVEI, Fax: 61259, ANDORRA LA VELLA

2001 JEAN PERISSE, C. Bearn, 12, Tel: 55497-55044, PAS DE LA CASA

ENTERTAINMENTS/EXCURSIONS

TOP SKI 7, C/. Engolasters, casa Jon, Tel: 31756-32503, Fax: 32384, ENCAMP

BEER SALOON

L'ORRI, Prat de la Creu, Tel: 27844, ANDORRA LA VELLA

DISCO

AMBIT, Erts, La Massana

CLICHE, Avda Tarragona, s/n, Tel: 25700, ANDORRA LA VELLA

OH ANDORRA, C/. La Llacuna, s/n, Tel: 22925, ANDORRA LA VELLA

PACHA, Baixada del Moli, Andorra la Vella

PUBS

VIDEO-MOTO Avda Co-Princep Episcopal, s/n, Casa Manel, 2, Tel: 32032, ENCAMP

MALIBU PUB Avda Tarragona. Urb Terra Vella, Tel: 61811, ANDORRA LA VELLA

FIRE SERVICE

Emergencies, Tel: 118; Services, Tel: 20020/55500

FISHING TACKLE & LICENSE INFORMATION

Refugi del Pescador, Av del Fener, 13, Escaldes.

GOVERNMENT/OFFICIAL NUMBERS

Andorra Govern Tel: 29345

Casa de la Vall	Tel: 21234
Oficina d' Immigracio	Tel: 26222
Vegueria episcopal	Tel: 20013
Vegueria francesa	Tel: 20809

HELICOPTER SERVICE

HELIAND SA, Xavier Goya, Prop., Offers air-taxi service to anywhere it can land. Their copter will carry up to five passengers and their luggage at approximately £700 per hour. Check with Government Tourist Office for its current phone number. Another agency: FORMOSA SERVEI D'HELICOPTERS, BAIXADA DEL MOLI, Estela 3, Andorra La Vella. Phone 60929 or 60088 or Fax: 60026

HOTELS

ANDORRA CENTER HOTEL, Carrer Dr Nequi 12, Tel: 24800/24999, Fax: 28329, ANDORRA LA VELLA

ANDORRA PARK HOTEL, Carrer Les Canals, Tel: 20979, Fax: 28329, ANDORRA LA VELLA

HOTEL BABOT, Crta. d'Ordino a Canillo, Tel: 35001, ORDINO

HOTEL BONA VISTA, Crta. de la Rabassa, Tel: 41231, SANT JULIA DE LORIA

HOTEL COMA PEDROSA, Arinsal, Andorra, Tel: 35123/36971, ARINSAL

HOTEL CORNELLA, Avda Meritxell, 61, Tel: 21480/21291, Tx: 341 AND CORSA Fax: 60240, ANDORRA LA VELLA

HOTEL CANUT, Avda Carlemany, 107, Tel: 21342 Tx: 398 AND, ESCALDES-ENGORDANY

HOTEL CONSELLER, Avda Miquel Mateu, 8, Tel: 21023, ESCALDES-ENGORDANY

HOTEL FESTA BRAVA, C/. La Llacuna, 7, Tel: 20741, ANDORRA LA VELLA

HOTEL FLORA, Antic Carrer Major, 23, Tel: 21508 - 21519 Tx: FLORATEL 209 AND, ANDORRA LA VELLA

HOTEL FONT DEL MARGE, Baixada del moli, 49, Tel: 23443 Fax: 23182, ANDORRA LA VELLA

GRAN HOTEL MARTICELLA, Avda Carlemany, 86, Tel: 20564/20681, ESCALDES-ENGORDANY

HOTEL LA MOLA, Avda Co-Princep Episcopal, 52, Tel: 31181, ENCAMP

HOTEL MOLA PARC, C/. Parc de la Mola, 5, Tel: 22811, ESCALDES-ENGORDANY

HOTEL PARIS-LONDRES, Avda Miquel Mateu, 3, Tel: 20814, ESCALDES-ENGORDANY

HOTEL POL, Avda Verge de CanXllch, 52, Tel: 41122 Tx: 272 AND, SANT JULIA DE LORIA

HOTEL LA PUBILLA, Avda Fiter I Rossell, 49, Tel: 20981, ESCALDES-ENGORDANY

PYRENEES HOTEL, Avda Princep Benlloch, Tel: 60006/20508/20398, Fax: 20265, ANDORRA LA VELLA

HOTEL RUTLLAN, Tel: 35000, Fax: 35180, LA MASSANA

HOTEL TIROL, Avda del Pessebre, 39, Tel: 21101, ESCALDES-ENGORDANY

APARTMENTS I RESIDENCIA, "COSMOS", Avda de les Escaldes, 10, Tel: 21927/21898, ESCALDES-ENGORDANY

HOTEL XALET RITZ, Prat dels Nogues, Sispony, Tel: 37877, Fax: 37720 LA MASSANA

INSURANCE

British companies with local offices include Commercial Union and a Lloyds Agency. Servissim handles the insurance for most English-speaking residents in Andorra and gets a special rate.

MAIL-DROP & MORE

After much searching for a reliable, well established outfit in Andorra, we recommend SERVISSIM, A COMPANY OFFERING THIS SPECIAL PACKAGE TO HILL REPORT READERS.

MONEY (FOREIGN EXCHANGE)

Day and night free information by phone 22000 & 22003

MEDICAL AND DENTAL SERVICES:

Emergencies:

CLINICA SANTA COLOMA, Carrer Gil Torres, Tel: 21905, ANDORRA LA VELLA

CLINICA VERGE DE MERITXELL, Avda Fiter i Rossell, Tel: 21521, ESCALDES-ENGORDANY

Psychiatrists

Dr Cabeza Jimenez Joan

Dr Cairat Vila Manel Antoni

Drop-in Medical Clinics

CLINICA VERGE DE MERITXELL, Avda. Fiter i Rossell, s/n, Tel: 23330, ESCALDES-ENGORDANY

CLINICA SANTA COLOMA, C/. Gil Torres, 15, Tel: 28880, ANDORRA LA VELLA

Gynaecology and Obstetrics Emergencies

CLINICA MERITXELL, Tel: 21521, ESCALDES-ENGORDANY

Dr GOUARRE Gerard, Ed. Claror, 4o - 3a, Tel: 27440, ESCALDES-ENGORDANY

Dr PUJOL FONOLLEDA Santiago, CLINICA MERITXELL, Tel: 23330, ESCALDES-ENGORDANY

Dr TOMAS ROCA Eduard, Avda. Princep Benlloch, 8, Tel: 23122, ANDORRA LA VELLA

Dr VILANOVA TRIAS Josep, Av Bra. Armengol 15, 1o, Tel: 20820, ANDORRA LA VELLA

Ophthamologist

Dr ROSSELL BRUN Eduard, Avda Meritxell, 207 - despatx 204, Tel: 60960, ANDORRA LA VELLA

Dentists

ENCAMP

Dr THIERRY Francesc, Avda Princep Benlloch, 4, Tel: 31957, PAS DE LA CASA

Dr SAUMUR Gerard, Edifici Malus Tel: 55208

ORDINO

Dr INGLES GASTELLO Joan C., Ed Casa Blanca Nova, Baixos dreta. Tel: 36448, ANDORRA LA VELLA

Dr DESTENAVE ARENY Miquel, C/. La Llacuna 2. Tel: 24118

Dr DIET Jean Marc, Avda Meritxell, 67. Tel: 22021

Dr KHAN LABOREL Silvia, Avda Meritxell 67. Tel: 22021

Dr KHOLER Hans Enric, C/. de l'Aigueta, 10. Tel: 22947

Dr PORQUERES GUITART Josep, C/. de l'Aigueta, 10. Tel: 22426

Dr SERRAT CABALLERIA Josep Ma., Baixada del Moli. Tel: 20097

SANT JULIA DE LORIA

Dr ROUSSEAU Gerard, Avda Verge de CanXlich, 55. Tel: 41315

Dr PARAHY Eric, Avda Verge de CanXlich 58. Tel: 42097

ESCALDES-ENGORDANY

Dr CASAL MOR Jaume, Ed. Salita Parc, Parc de la Mola. Tel: 21051

Dr DUONG Antoni, C/. Nou-Ed. Nou Park. Tel: 21038

Dr FORTO NOGUERA Antoni, Avda del Fener. Tel: 23762

Dr LEIGHTON, Placa Co-Princeps, 7. Tel: 20947

Dr MARCELLY Daniel, C/. Pare Enric Graner, 2. Tel: 27114

Dr RABANAL SUAREZ J.L., C/. Sant Antoni, 1. Tel: 21712

Dr BALDRICH LLORT MercQ, C/. La Sardana. Tel: 26459

Occupational Therapists

Dra. ALEIX TUGAS Josiana, C/. La Lacuna, 1, Tel: 27608, ANDORRA LA VELLA

Dra BERNE CALBO Nuria, C/. Bra. Riberaygua, 11, Tel: 28219, ANDORRA LA VELLA

Dra DARTIGUELONGE, Liliana, C/Sant Antoni, 1, Tel: 22505, ESCALDES-ENGORDANY

Dr FROGER Daniel, C/la UniS, 2, Tel: 21540, ANDORRA LA VELLA

Dr HERRANZ PALOMO Josep, C/la Llacuna 7, Tel: 20741, ANDORRA LA VELLA

CLINICA SANTA COLOMA, C/Gil Torres 15, Tel: 21905, ANDORRA LA VELLA

Medical Doctors/General Practitioners

ENCAMP

Dr PALLARES DARSA Manel, Avda Co-Princep FrancVs, 23, Tel: 31114, PAS DE LA CASA

Dr ESCODA SALES Josep, Consultori MVdic-QuirTrgic, Edifici ResidVncia. Tel: 55225

ORDINO

Dra PEREZ SERRA Rosa, Placa Major, Casa Nova Comu. Tel: 36636

LA MASSANA

Dr ALDOSA MORA Josep, Casa Gabriel, 1er. 3a. Tel: 35657

Dra MASARDO Margarida, Casa Armengol, 3er. 3a. Tel: 36556

Dr VERDAGUER FERRE Jordi, Casa Armengol, 3er. 3a. Tel: 36557

ANDORRA LA VELLA

Dr ALONSO FRIAS Claudi, Prada Guillamo, Ed. Oros, 1er. 3a. Tel: 20543

Dr BREIL Joan Francesc, Avda Meritxell, 112-2on. 2a. Tel: 21411

Dr BUSQUETS BUSQUETS Jordi, Prada Guillamo, Ed. Oros, 1er. 1a. Tel: 20862

Dra. ILLESCAS BERMEJO Julia, C/. Babot Camp, 4. Tel: 28258

Dr RUIZ GARCIA Antoni, Avda. Princep Benlloch, 8. Tel: 21668

SANT JULIA DE LORIA

Dra. BATLLE JORDANA Roser, Casa Molines, 2a principal. Tel: 42724

Dr BOUDE Thierry, Casa Molines, 2a Principal. Tel: 42724

Dr DURO FARRAS Josep, Avda Verge de CanXlich, 39 1er. Tel: 41078

Dra. FITER VILAJOANA Meri, C/. Doctor Palau, 44. Tel: 41290

Dr LOPEZ PINACHO Timoteu, C/. Doctor Palau, 44. Tel: 41290

Dra. PONS CALDERON Emma, C/. Doctor Palau, 44. Tel: 41290

ESCALDES-ENGORDANY

Dr BURGUES MONTSERRAT Josep, Avda. Carlemany, 18 3er. Tel: 60840

Dr BUSGUES MONTSERRAT LluRs, Avda Carlemany, 95 1er. Tel: 20761

Dr CASAL MOR Jacint, Avda Carlemany, 71 1er. 1a. Tel: 27567

Dr. PLA BUREU Albert, Avda Carlemany, 71 1er. 1a. Tel: 27567

Dr SANCHEZ CLAVER, Joan, Avda Carlemany, 71 1er. 1a. Tel: 27567

CANILLO

Dr VIDAL VIDAL, Joan Carles, Cal Metge. Tel: 51050

Infants Paediatric Services (Infants) Emergencies

CLINICA MERITXELL. Tel: 21521

Dr ALBOS MARTINEZ Joan

CLINICA MERITXELL, Tel: 23330, ESCALDES- ENGORDANY

Dra. BARO MORTES Carme, Ed. Claror, 4o. 4a, Tel: 27440, ESCALDES-ENGORDANY

Dr DIAZ ROSAS, C/. de la Borda, Tel: 21634, ANDORRA LA VELLA

Dra DONCEL JAEN Carme, Roc dels Escolls, 3-5 C, Tel: 23093, ANDORRA LA VELLA

Dr RIBO JORDANA Pau, C/. de les Canals, Tel: 20212, ANDORRA LA VELLA

PHARMACIES

CANILLO

FARMACIA ABARSET, Carretera General. Tel: 51540

ENCAMP

FARMACIA D'ENCAMP, Avda Co-Princep Episcopal, 3. Tel: 31227

FARMACIA TORRENT, Av Co. Episcopal. Tel: 32660

FARMACIA MUXELLA, Av Co. Episcopal.

FARMACIA BAIXENCH, C/Major, Casa Marxanda. Tel: 32732

PAS DE LA CASA

FARMACIA DEL PAS, C/. Major Edifici Borra. Tel: 55160

ORDINO

FARMACIA d'ORDINO, Carretera General. Tel: 35283

LA MASSANA

FARMACIA LA MASSANA, Casa Nova Sabater. Tel: 35242

ANDORRA LA VELLA

FARMACIA NOVA, Adva Santa Coloma Edifici Ribalta. Tel: 25688

FARMACIA ENCLAR, Avda Princep Benlloch, 87. Tel: 24419

FARMACIA FENERS, Av Bra. Riberaugua 2. Tel: 61761

FARMACIA MERITXELL, C/.Dr. Nequi. Tel: 26060

FARMACIA MITJAVILA, Avda Princep Benlloch, 6. Tel: 20224

FARMACIA TRES CREUS, C/. les Canals, 5. Tel: 20212

FARMACIA INTERNACIONAL, Avda Meritxell, 16. Tel: 20162

FARMACIA DEL PONT, Avda Meritxell, 68. Tel: 21352

FARMACIA ROSSELLA, Avda Meritxell, 43. Tel: 21954

FARMACIA PASTEUR, Avda Meritxell, 84. Tel: 20785

FARMACIA CENTRAL, Avda Riberaygua, 20. Tel: 32993

GRAN FARMACIA, Avda Riberaygua, 53. Tel: 28009

FARMACIA SANTA COLOMA, Av d'Enclar, 70. Tel: 20613 (Santa Coloma)

POLICE

Emergencies, Tel: 110; Services, Tel: 21222

PROPERTY MANAGEMENT COMPANIES

CASA SERVEI SL, Carretera General, Tel: 35633, Fax: 37428, LA MASSANA

CISA SERVEI, see CISA

SERVISSIM, see Servissim entry under Mail Drop

RED CROSS

Tel: 25225

RENT-A-CAR:

AVIS, Av d'Enclar, 140, Santa Coloma, Tel: 63555

EUROPCAR, at Hotel Roc Blanc, Escaldes. Tel: 60650

HERTZ, at Pyrenees Department Store. Tel: 60414

SERVEIS TURISTICS SA, C/. Dr. Vilanova, s/n Tel: 29303, ANDORRA LA VELLA

RELIGIOUS SERVICES

As Andorra is one of the last feudal religious states in the world, only the official church (Catholic) is permitted to operate openly. There is a monthly English language service at the Parish Church of La Massana, permitted by the Bishop under special licence. Details from Gil Lamb, tel 35258, or John Bishop, tel 37156. During our visits we did not notice any announcements for services of other faiths. Perhaps readers would write to us on the subject of alternative religious services for inclusion in our next edition. Every town in Andorra has at least one Catholic church with an extensive program of masses, vigils, Sunday schools and musical events.

RESTAURANTS

EL ARENYS (Pizzeria), Crta. General, tel: 51427, CANILLO

LA BODEGUILLA, C/. Alzinaret, 3, ANDORRA LA VELLA

LA BORDA DE L'AVI, Crta. d'Arinsal, tel: 35154, LA MASSANA

CAN MANEL, C/. Mestre Xavier Planes, s/n, tel: 22397, ANDORRA LA VELLA

CAN PERE, Casa Jumpere, tel 35415, ANYOS

EL CANDELER, C/ Cap del Poble, s/n, tel: 26787, BANTA COLOMA

CASA CANUT, Avda. Carlemany, 107, tel: 21342, ESCALDES

CASA NONO, ANYOS

CAN LLEONARD, Avda. Tarragona. Ed. Terra Vella, tel: 61032, ANDORRA LA VELLA

CELLER D'EN TONI, C/Verge del Pilar, 4, tel: 21843/21252, tx: CELLTONI, ANDORRA LA VELLA

LES COSTES DE GIBERGA, Crta. d'Ordino, s/n, tel: 35110, LA MASSANA

LA CULTIA, Av del Fener s/n, tel: 61700, ESCALDES

L'HORT DEL CAMP, Urb. Mirador d'Emcamp, 13, tel: 32624, ENCAMP

ELS CRANCS, (Restaurant-Cafeteria-Pizzeria), C/l'Alzinaret, 9, tel: 23929, ANDORRA LA VELLA

EL FAISA, Cap del Carrer, 4, tel: 20394, ANDORRA LA VELLA

EL GRAN CAFE, tel: 26122, ESCALDES

FONT DEL MARGE, Baixada del Moli, 49, tel: 23443, ANDORRA LA VELLA

TRATTORIA MAMA, Av. del Fener, s/n, tel: 61700, ESCALDES

LA MASIA, Av. de Salou, s/n, tel: 22366, SANTA COLOMA

L'ORRI, Prat de la Creu, tel: 27844, ANDORRA LA VELLA

EL MOLI DEL PEANO, tel: 51258, CANILLO

MOLI DELS FANALS, C/Dr. Vilanova, s/n, tel: 21381 & 24381, ANDORRA LA VELLA

EL MOLI DE LA PLACA, Crta. d'Arinsal, tel: 35281, ARINSAL

NICA, Cap del Carrer, 2, tel: 20825, ANDORRA LA VELLA

PASTA I VI, Avda. Riberaygua, 53, tel: 28908, ANDORRA LA VELLA

EL PI (Restaurant-Pizzeria), Av. Co-Princep Episcopal, s.n, tel: 31394, ENCAMP

ELS PINS, C/ la Llacuna, 19, tel: 22631, ANDORRA LA VELLA

PRAT GRAN, Crta Coll D'Ordino, tel: 35130, ORDINO

LOU PIZZAIOLO, Avda. Dr. Mitjavila, 36, tel: 20639, ANDORRA LA VELLA

SANT MALO, (Restaurant-Creperia-Grill), Promendade Riu Valira, Darrera Av. Co-Princep de Gaulle, tel: 28795, ESCALDES

TABERNA DEL MALLOL, C/ Verge del Pilar, 6, tel: 25199, ANDORRA LA VELLA

RESTAURANT TELECADIRA, Crta del Tremat, Ed. Telecabina, tel: 31744, ENCAMP

VALIRA - Camping, Avda. de Salou, s/n, tel: 24254, ANDORRA LA VELLA

EL VIETNAM, Avda. Tarragona, 1, tel: 21917, ANDORRA LA VELLA

EL XALET, Crta. General, s/n, tel: 35068, ERTS

RESTAURANT XALET, LA MASSANA

XENIUS, Avda. Francesc Cairat, s/n, tel: 42454, SANT JULIA DE LORIA

XOPLUC, Crta. General de Sispony, tel: 35645, SISPONY

SHOPPING CENTERS

Monsa Commercial Center and Supermarket, Av Carlemany, Escaldes Center Commercial Forum, Av Carlemany 36, Escaldes Hipo Commercial Center, Saint Julia De Loria Also, see section on Shopping in this report. These (above) tend to be huge warehouse-like discount houses specializing in a wide range of the most popular tourist exports. All tend to be cheaper for generic (non-brand) goods than Pyrenees Department store, which carries more designer labels, named brands, and upmarket goods, at discounts.

SERVISSIM

See "Mail Drop". Special Category. Describing themselves as "Your Agent in Andorra" Servissim provides a wide variety of services. See listing under Mail Drop & More.
We give our highest recommendation to: **Simon Binsted, General Manager-Servissim, SL, Roc Escolls 3-4 A., Ave Meritxell, 20, Andorra la Vella, Principat d'Andorra, tel (33-628) 60414 or 61148, fax: (33-628) 63797**
CISA-SERVEI, Ed La Cabanota, La Massana, tel 35196 (only for clients of CISA)

TAKE AWAY FOOD

PASTA I VI, C/. Bonaventura Riberaygua, 53, Tel: 28 9 08, ANDORRA LA VELLA
EL BON TIBERI, Crta de la Massana, casa Pascal, Tel: 37 4 09, LA MASSANA
FOTOBIP, Avda Meritxell, 8, Magatzems Pyrenees - Planta baixa, Tel: 28 0 76, ANDORRA LA VELLA
McDONALDS, Av. Meritxell, 105 ANDORRA LA VELLA

TOURIST OFFICES:

Good for free maps and brochures and hotel reservations. They are located in the main commercial sections of every town. Tourist offices abroad: Paris, Barcelona

TOURISM

SYNDICAT D'INICIATIVA DE LES VALLS

D'ANDORRA

Tel: 20214

TRAVEL AGENCIES

AMERICAN EXPRESS agent, Viatges Relax, Roc Escolls, Andorra la Vella, tel 22044

ANDORRA TOURS, C/. Joan Maragall, s/n - Ed. Capri, entressol 1a, tel: 29210, ANDORRA LA VELLA

CASH ANDORRA, Av Dr. Vilanova - Ed. Thais, 2 D, tel: 29274, ANDORRA LA VELLA

INTERNOVA, Avda Riberaygua, 25 5a B, tel: 28604, ANDORRA LA VELLA

PARADORES DE ESPANA, SERVEIS TURISTICS S/A, C/. Dr. Vilanova, s/n Ed Thais, tel: 29303, ANDORRA LA VELLA

TOP SKI 7, C/Engolasters, casa Jon, tel: 31756/32503, ENCAMP

TURIVAC-TURISME I VACANCES, C/. Alzinaret, 12, tel: 29333, ANDORRA LA VELLA

DO YOU NEED A CONSULTANCY?

Scope can offer you the services of several expert consultants who will answer your questions and advise you equally well.

Indeed, we would say that the consultants we are now using, have been recommended by Dr Hill because they are engaged in actually putting into effect the advice which they offer.

The first, Peter Thompson is a PT whose specialities include knowledge of worldwide company incorporation and advice, maildrops in various parts of the world and imaginative answers to legal, accountancy and tax questions including the kind of advice that you *really* want to know. He also has many useful connections around the world.

If you have any general PT type questions or require advice in the areas mentioned above then we highly recommend Peter. His consultancy fee is £200 for a letter, fax or telephone consultation plus the cost of the call; or £700 (US $1250) for half a day (four hours) plus travel costs according to where you require him to go, or you may visit him in Europe where he is often to be found. If you can arrange to meet in the same country that Peter is in at a particular time, or wait until he is going there, travelling expenses will be minimal or nil.

Please send your written consultancy together with cheque, cash or draft payable to Peter Thompson to Scope International Ltd, 62 Murray Road, Waterlooville, PO8 9JL, UK, and we will forward it on immediately. If you require a personal consultation, please telephone our office on 0705 (+44 705 overseas) 592255, and we will arrange a convenient appointment on behalf of Peter Thompson and yourself.

If you need to discuss confidential movement of funds, bearer shares, secret numbered bank accounts, or simply financial secrecy with minimum risk of loss or disclosure, then Robert Stirling could be your ideal consultant. He leads an international group of currency and banking specialists and has great experience in legal world currency movement.

If you would like to discuss your particular requirements with Robert Stirling, arrangements can be made through Scope. The fee is £700 for a half day (4 hours) plus travel and associated costs.

If your consultancy is of an immigration or passport nature then we recommend an immigration specialist who can offer you a passport and immigration consultancy. He can also arrange second passports on your behalf in a variety of countries as well as offer diplomatic passports and honorary consulates.

If you would like a consultancy with an international immigration specialist, please send £200 (US $350) together with your written questions and as much background information as you can provide, and we will forward this for direct reply from our international immigration consultant. If you would just like to receive further information on the services that our immigration consultants can offer, please write to Scope International and we will advise you.

How do you get the coveted "green card"? What kind of visa do you need in order to study, train, set up a business, work as a domestic, perform or write in the United States? Miles Cavendish, our specialist US immigration consultant will be able to answer all your questions, and some you won't have even known to ask! His initial fee is £50/US $80.

If you are looking to come to the UK, we can offer you the exclusive services of a UK based immigration consultant who will give you a brief consultation by letter for just £85/US $150. Both specialists have extensive experience in handling respective applications directly up to the highest levels.

If in doubt as to which consultant you need, please ring Scope and discuss the nature of the advice you seek and we will be able to advise you.

Please note that before spending money on consultations, you will invariably find it cheaper to read the specialised Scope Reports which deal with particular subjects (especially *PT*) because the answer is probably within. It is much cheaper and cost effective for you to obtain information from the Scope Special Reports than from a personalised response. Reading *PT1* and *PT2* may also make you think about avenues of which you have never thought about previously. We advise you to read this Report and *The Passport Report* and to think carefully about the nature of your questions and what you wish to achieve before requesting a consultancy in order to maximise its benefit.

OTHER REPORTS PUBLISHED by SCOPE INTERNATIONAL LTD.

PT 1 – THE PERPETUAL TRAVELLER
A COHERENT PLAN FOR A STRESS-FREE, HEALTHY AND PROSPEROUS LIFE WITHOUT GOVERNMENT INTERFERENCE, TAXES OR COERCION
4th Edition
by Dr. W.G. Hill

PT stands for Prepared Thoroughly, Perpetual Tourist, Prior Taxpayer and much, much more.

People of intelligence and wealth owe it to themselves and their descendants to have five 'flags'. No one with common sense should give all their assets or allegiance to just one flag. Why? Because no country nor any government has ever survived more than a few generations without totally annihilating itself or its own middle and upper classes. Even in that 'last bastion of capitalism', the USA, people of property were thrice forced to flee the country. In 1775, one third (the entire middle and ruling class), was forced to move to Canada; these were the Tories who supported England in the Revolution. In 1865, it happened again; all large land owners (who supported the Confederacy in the Civil War) were forced to migrate to Mexico, Europe or South America. In the post 1917 period, prohibition, confiscatory taxes, compulsory military service, and suffocating government regulations once again caused wealthy Americans (and Europeans) to seek new flags. **Five million of the wealthiest and most productive Americans now live abroad.** Eighty-five percent of all liquid private wealth is already anonymously registered 'offshore'. CAN YOU AFFORD TO HAVE ONLY ONE FLAG? - NOT IF YOUR NET WORTH IS OVER US$ 250,000.

THE FIVE FLAGS OF THE PT

Flag 1. BUSINESS BASE. These are the places where you make your money. They must be different from the place where you 'legally reside', your personal fiscal domicile. Your business base should be in a place that gives a tax holiday to your business, freedom from over-regulation, and good access to contacts, labour markets or materials needed for conducting your business. London, Tokyo, and New York are the Big Apples for Finance and Insurance. Zurich, Hong Kong, Singapore, Frankfurt and Milan are among the second-rank contenders.

Flag 2. PASSPORT AND CITIZENSHIP. These should be from a country unconcerned about its offshore citizens or what they do outside its borders. There must be no tax or military requirement for non-residents. PASSPORTS MUST BE AVAILABLE TO FOREIGNERS.

Flag 3. DOMICILE. This should be a tax haven with good communications; a place where wealthy, productive people can be creative, live, relax, prosper and enjoy themselves, preferably with bank secrecy and no threat of war or revolution. Monaco, Campione, The Channel Islands, Andorra, Bermuda, Thailand and Gibraltar are all recommended.

Flag 4. ASSET REPOSITORY. This should be a place from which assets, securities and business affairs can be managed by proxy. Requirements are: The availability of highly competent financial managers, confidential banking, no taxes on non-residents, or non-citizens. One of the best places in which to plant your fourth flag would be Liechtenstein. Other possibilities would be Austria, Luxembourg, Switzerland, New York or London.

Flag 5. PLAYGROUNDS. These are places where you would actually physically spend your time. Normally, because of legal restrictions on how long one may stay without being inducted as a taxpayer, it is necessary to have from two to four playgrounds. One might try to avoid spending more than 90 days per year in any one of them. We look for quality of life. **For 'no nukes' and good fishing:** New Zealand. **For the most interesting sex life imaginable:** Thailand, Costa Rica or the Philippines. **Superb climate:** California. **Best food:** French Riviera or Hong Kong. **Stimulating cities:** Paris, London, San Francisco. **To buy the best things at the cheapest prices:** Singapore, Hong Kong (or Denmark, for cars).

PT fully explains all Five Flags. It is a complete guide to getting the most out of life that this Earth can offer. Each individual should have at least two, but ideally three toeholds in each 'flag'. For example:

1. A BUSINESS OR SOURCE OF INCOME IN New York, London and Singapore.
2. A PASSPORT FROM Canada, Brazil, Italy and Australia.
3. A LEGAL OR FISCAL ADDRESS IN Monaco, Campione or the Channel Islands.
4. A BANK ACCOUNT OR OTHER ASSETS REGISTERED ANONYMOUSLY IN Liechtenstein trusts or foundations.
5. FRIENDS AND FUN IN Paris, Bangkok, Manila, Buenos Aires, Sydney and San Francisco.

ISBN 0 906619 24 6.

How to do it? . . . Read *PT – The Perpetual Traveller,* available from Scope International Ltd, 62 Murray Road, Waterlooville, Hampshire PO8 9JL, UK. Price – £60 UK Sterling (or equivalent) by credit card, cash, cheque or banker's draft. Price includes postage and packing, and please allow 6-8 weeks for surface delivery outside UK. For quicker air mail add £15 or equivalent (allow 3-4 weeks for delivery). Ordering details and order form are supplied on the last two pages of this Report.

REMEMBER: Consultations with specialists are available to all purchasers and our no nonsense money back guarantee applies to all our publications.

PT 2

THE PRACTICE: FREEDOM AND PRIVACY TACTICS FOR THE NINETIES – AND BEYOND

1st Edition, NEW for 1993

by Dr. W.G. Hill

Now is the time to take proper precautions, says W.G. Hill, father of P.T. and the world's leading expert on personal tax havens, in this startling book. Contrary to the popular image projected by mainstream media and most governments, your taxes are shooting up and your personal freedom is being taken away, bit by bit. Anyone with a visible pocket will become a victim. The most dangerous place on earth is wherever *you* are. But in this hands-on guide to low profile and privacy, PT-style, W.G. Hill shows you how to regain your lost freedom. In more than 200 fact-filled pages, he teaches you the little-known tactics and techniques of living tax free. For the first time ever in print, he gives away all his privacy secrets and shares with you unique insights on how to escape what he terms "the scam called government". This explosive volume deals with matters that no other books ever dared in a practical, hands-on manner. You will learn all the world's unknown ins and outs of getting, and keeping, a life free from problems, frustrations, harrassment, extortion, lawsuits and the implications and ramifications of all of these – the works.

DO YOU HAVE THE ESSENTIAL KNOWLEDGE FOR A FREE LIFE?
Answer these simple questions to determine if you have the information and tools necessary for a rich life in complete freedom:

* Do you know the world's six best ways to transfer cash across borders? Do you know how to triple your interest earnings and gain when currencies change?
* Do you have a collection of untraceable credit cards? Do you have foreign credit cards in a selection of names other than your own?
* Do you know the how-to of no-name bank accounts, where ID is not needed?
* Can you name the ten best low profile mail tips? Do you have a "dead drop"?
* Do you own and operate at least one PT—PC in a foreign jurisdiction?
* Will you be able to keep your money safe despite the coming world tax-squad, the new OECD treaties and the international laws already in place? Do you even know all the dangers of the nineties and beyond? Are you willing to run the risk of asset stripping and long jail sentences for a "crime" you did not commit' a so-called crime invented by money-grabbing world governments?

If you answered "no" to one or more of these questions, please do not waste any time in getting *PT 2,* the all-new 1993 tome for tax exiles and perpetual travellers. In five lengthy parts, W.G. Hill thoroughly covers ALL privacy and low profile questions – even those you never dared ask. From such simple things as securing your cars or using all the unknown loopholes of air travel, Hill firmly moves on to invisible ink 1993-style, crossing borders *sans* passports and what he calls the Ten Privacy Tenets. This book even gives you the inside facts of essential low profile gadgets and some privacy paraphernalia that would probably be illegal if your government knew that they existed!

Contents also include... True, tried and tested: W.G. Hill's own telephone tactics, now with a PT shortlist for phone secrecy... All about mobile phones, Super Phones, add-on gadgets for your phones... How best to transmit faxes... The art of compartmentalizing your life... Never-before-told maildrop secrets... Secure communications... Also: The secret trust, onshore or offshore? And so much, much more. **Stop Press:** This volume now comes complete with a bonus – W.G. Hill's complete guide to banking worldwide, including some secret, supersafe havens for smart money only. Plus a complete course in bearer shares and bonds.

In his introduction, Dr W.G. Hill writes: *This book is dedicated to showing people of intelligence how to stay FREE in every sense of the word. While you may consider yourself a "free man" (or woman), chances are that you are not. The bad news is that even if you are currently living a fairly normal and happy life, events may conspire to turn against you and wind up stealing your money, your freedom – and ultimately, your life. Today, you are a sitting duck – unless you take precautions now. The good news, on the other hand, is that there are plenty of things that you may do yourself to thwart whatever dangers are likely to pop up – in advance, and with just a modicum of effort and expense.* Are you ready for true, undiluted, unrestrained freedom in all personal and financial matters?

Do you believe that "an ounce of preparation is worth about a ton of cure"? If so *PT 2 ("The Practice")* is for you. If you are not content just "letting things happen" then it makes perfect sense to make sure that they don't – or, if they still do, that this will not be to your extreme disadvantage.

ISBN 0 906619 40-8.

PT 2 is available from Scope International Ltd., 62 Murray Road, Waterlooville, Hampshire PO8 9JL, UK. Price – £60 UK Sterling (or equivalent) by credit card, cash, cheque or banker's draft. Price includes postage and packing, and please allow 6-8 weeks for surface delivery outside UK. For quicker air mail service add £15 or equivalent (allow 3-4 weeks for delivery). Ordering details and order form are supplied on the last two pages of this Report.

Right now, in his brand new first edition of the PT-sequel, W.G. Hill gives you the low down, no-nonsense, straight facts about how to set up those seemingly elusive safeguards that may shield you in times of trouble. If you put the information in this book to practical use you will find that you, too, can keep your money, your freedom and your life. And forever be Home Free, PT.

REMEMBER: Personal consultations are available to all purchasers and our no nonsense money back guarantee applies to all our publications.

THE PASSPORT REPORT
HOW TO LEGALLY OBTAIN A SECOND FOREIGN PASSPORT
8th Edition
by Dr. W.G. Hill

Why entrust your life and your freedom to any one government? Politicians regard you as an expendable national resource, but *you* do not 'belong' to any one country if you hold several passports and nationalities.

A second passport ensures mobility. Millions of individuals would be alive today if they'd had second passports before the holocaust in Germany, and repression in Argentina, Cambodia, and many other countries.

Many countries now 'sell' passports. The wording of their laws describe entrepreneurs, financial benefactors, treaty traders, and special investors in government loan paper as being welcomed new citizens. But the bottom line is the same: put up from $10,000 to $100,000 and you can obtain an almost instant passport. Other countries offer instant citizenship if your ancestors were nationals, or if you are of a certain race or religion: Thailand if you are Buddhist, Israel if you are Jewish, Lebanon if you are a displaced Moslem. Almost anyone can qualify for a free passport, and anyone with about $15,000 can have a choice of several more. *The Passport Report* closely examines the official and unofficial channels in more than 50 countries.

Citizenship can now also be thought of as a business proposition. But what countries offer more advantages? What are the net costs? Taxes, investment opportunities, travel restrictions, financial privacy, social values and retirement are only a few valid considerations closely examined in this Special Report.

A Second Passport could save your life, your money and your freedom. The key to this option is your new passport. Specifically, your 'second' passport, one which you can obtain from another country. This valuable document can open opportunities you never thought possible and provide 'back doors' that could literally save your life. The reason governments don't make it easy or publicise such options is that they are concerned with controlling and taxing their own citizens, and could regard popularisation of second passport procural as a threat to 'national security'.

Most countries have well established, but little-known, procedures for issuing passports under circumstances which most observers would regard as loopholes. It is knowledge of these 'exceptions' which allows intrepid individuals to obtain multiple foreign passports, and thus choose the countries most suitable for their purposes.

Put another way, *it is perfectly legal* to obtain several foreign passports so long as one knows the special rules for their issuance. It is of course legal and possible for citizens of most countries to obtain one or more passports without giving up their present citizenship, even though the widespread belief is that certain countries do not permit dual nationality. Yet approximately 10 per cent of the populations of countries like South Africa and United States of America currently legally hold dual nationality. How dual nationality can be obtained legally is fully explained. In many situations there is no residence requirement, and in a few places there is *never* even any need to visit.

Since the special rules involved are certainly not publicised by most foreign ministries, we have been fortunate in receiving this special report by international attorney and consultant, Dr. W.G. Hill. *The Passport Report* is unquestionably the most detailed and comprehensive guide on this subject, and we are pleased to be able to offer it to you.

Here is a brief overview of the contents of *The Passport Report:*

* The first step: psychological preparation.
* Those who advertise and claim to provide second passports.
* How to determine which passport suits you best.
* 100 countries examined in detail.
* Eliminating taxes with your second passport.
* Indirect routes ('back doors').
* Documents usable in lieu of passports.
* Should you hire a lawyer or agency?
* Instant passports and how to get them.
* Non-citizen passports; Diplomatic and service passports; Refugee passports; Provisional passports; Honorary passports.
* Dual nationality: problems and benefits.
* Actual case histories detailing exactly how individuals went about securing second passports. Most informative!

This report will open your eyes to many ideas and options you've never thought of before. More significantly, it will allow you to realistically appraise the risks of not having a second passport and assets properly placed to enable you to escape, survive and prosper. War, revolutions, political changes, personal economic reverses are all possible, if not inevitable at some time or another. Are you prepared?

The Passport Report provides referrals to foreign specialists for additional assistance, and consultancies are available to all purchasers. You will find *The Passport Report* to be an invaluable guide.

With over 300 pages packed with unique and vital information, *The Passport Report* is the most detailed and useful book of its kind. Our no nonsense money back guarantee applies if it does not deliver more usable and accurate information than any other report on the same subject, at any price.

The Passport Report is available from Scope International Ltd. Price £60.00. See last two pages in this report for ordering details.

ISBN 0 906619 19 X

THINK LIKE A TYCOON
HOW TO MAKE A MILLION OR MORE IN THREE YEARS OR LESS!
THE TIMELESS CLASSIC BESTSELLER
3rd Edition
by Dr. W.G. Hill

Do you sincerely want to be rich without knocking yourself out? Do you want respect? Do you need love?

Learn the incredible secret that will bring you the *happiness only money can buy.*

You CAN become a millionaire in three years or less while, at the same time, having three times more fun out of life. Of course you are sceptical. So read on.

My name is W.G. Hill. I did not make my millions (like some authors) by writing books about things I have not done myself personally. Starting from scratch, without money, special skills, contacts or luck I founded eight totally unrelated part-time FUN businesses. I saw **each** of them earn me over a million Pounds **each** in three years or less.

While I was making all this money, I managed to go to an average of five parties a week, plus two or three concerts, plays or movies. **SEX!** My love life didn't suffer either – as I had more "companionship" in a year than most men have in a lifetime. What was the sex-appeal secret of a grumpy, overweight, middle-aged bald guy with crooked teeth and thick glasses? **I was doing things that appeared exciting and glamorous to women. I *was* the action and they *came* to me.** There is no Aphrodisiac that comes anywhere close to the appeal of **MONEY** and **POWER!**

When thousands of people depend upon you economically, some will fawn and dote upon your every word. Some try to gain your good will with gifts, sexual favors, bribes and offers you can't refuse. *When you can refuse, you know that you have arrived.* When you can go to the best restaurants in town with your friends and order anything you fancy without considering the price, when you can travel the world free as a bird, you know that you have ARRIVED! If you can *live anywhere* in the world, have any partners and friends you want, Tell off or ignore government bureaucracy, union officials, politicians and former bosses, then you know that you have found FREEDOM!

With money, everything else will fall into place. *Try it!*

Would you trade your present life for what I have just described? Then read on. Years ago I was broke, physically in bad shape and seriously in debt. Then I found concealed in a window box a dusty tattered old book. It had been hidden in the summer cottage of my close friend's father. He was a very rich and powerful man. Later on I discovered that he owed his good fortune to his own discovery of this book many years earlier. Reading the timeless volume I discovered an amazing formula that every single super-rich person seems to have used to gain wealth. It was so incredibly easy to understand that I started to apply it within twenty four hours. In six months I was a millionaire. I never had to work again.

In Chapter One I learned how to avoid mistakes that keep 94 per cent of the population just plodding along in a miserable rut – dissatisfied with everything. In Chapter Two I discovered how to "Think Like a Tycoon" – how to set and achieve goals. Chapter Three taught me how to *achieve these goals quickly* – not by moving up some corporate ladder for 30 years. I saw how to make things happen *fast* plus how to strike it very big in two or three years (at the most). Chapter Four taught me how to use credit and borrow unlimited funds (usually interest free) from bankers and investors. Another important chapter told me why all the "investments" I thought of as sound are really only for suckers.

Although the book I read was written two hundred years earlier, it was like Aladdin's Magic Lamp for me and changed my life dramatically. After two hours of reading I never earned less than a million a year for the next 30 years. Other millionaires went up and down like a yo-yo, but I just kept having more and more fun by getting richer and richer.

Now after many adventures, at the age of 49 I have retired (in great comfort I might add) to write my memoirs. Before doing so I wanted to pass on to other ambitious lads the age-old secrets that made me a millionaire at the age of 24.

I took the original timeless secrets of wealth, transformed them into modern English and added my own experiences and witty humor. Then I tested out the formula on my best friend, a poverty stricken but talented jazz musician. Let's call my buddy "Warren Trumpet". For years my friend had been insisting that he sincerely wanted to be very rich. I gave him the manuscript of my book. In six months he was a millionaire. In two years more he had gross annual earnings of over FOUR MILLION DOLLARS. As a jazz musician, even with a hit record, *The Girl From Ipanema,* he had never earned more than twenty thousand a year. Warren never had much of an IQ. A highschool dropout, he used to read and write like a ten year old. But that didn't stop him from using my unpublished manuscript to become one of the richest men in the world.

If he can do it, you can do it.

Truth is, I'd like to give away these secrets. If everyone used them, the world would be a richer, more productive and happy place. But I learned from the SPCA (Society for Prevention of Cruelty to Animals) that if you give away a puppy dog, that dog is more likely to be mistreated and kicked around than if you *SELL* that same dog for $100.

I want to give you respect, value and seriously apply this incredible, exciting formula. *I will not give it to you for free.* On the back page is the order form you must complete and send to Scope International now, if you want to get a copy of my sumptuously bound, gold blocked, limited edition of ***Think Like A Tycoon. How to Make a Million or More in Three Years or Less.*** (Personal registered copy, not for resale).

ISBN 0 906619 30 0

THE CAMPIONE REPORT
SWITZERLAND'S SECRET SEMI-TROPICAL TAX HAVEN
4th Edition
by Dr. W.G. Hill

W.G. Hill, the world's leading expert on personal tax havens predicts that Campione, a strange accident of history, anomaly of geography and climatic freak, will be one of the most fashionable tax havens of the next decade.

This report shows anyone how to become a legal resident of this soon-to-be discovered enclave of the super-rich. *Campione is a unique semi-autonomous community located entirely within Switzerland.* But as a separate country, it is **not subject to any Swiss laws, taxes or tax treaties**. Strange as it may seem, becoming a resident of Campione gives one all the advantages of being Swiss, but none of the disadvantages. No compulsory lifetime military camps, no heavy Swiss income taxes, none of the disadvantages of being (as Switzerland is) *outside* the European Community.

Campione is a part of the EC with all the benefits of passport free, visa free travel. Its citizens have the right to travel, work, engage in commerce or perform services anywhere in the EC. Best of all, Campione has "in practice" no income taxes. This Special Report shows you how to achieve these tax benefits even without acquiring residency.

Campione also is one of the few places in the EC where there is no VAT (value added tax), which seriously reduces the price of goods and services.

The Campione Report tells all the secrets, but here's some more highlights:

Campione enjoys a freak Mediterranean climate found only in the small Italian Swiss Province of Ticino, where Campione is located. Because it is on lovely Lake Lugano and considerably lower in altitude than the rest of mountainous Switzerland, it's white sand beach supports a small grove of tropical palm trees. Your 'sea-view' villa in Campione will be gently caressed by balmy yet non-humid tropical breezes. However, although Campione is in a 'Banana Belt', nearby ski slopes are clearly visible. Half an hour on the local funicular railway takes you up to the powder runs!

The cost of living is less than half that of Monte Carlo, Paris, London or New York. There is no pollution, industry or crime. The mountain and lake scenery is breathtaking. The sub-Alpine climate and year-round temperature is second to none. A vibrant social and cultural life is a few minutes away in Lugano or Locarno by regular ferry boat. Take the superhighway due south from Campione and in forty five minutes you can hear the world's best grand opera at La Scala or visit the fabulous shops of downtown Milan. There are more bankers and stockbrokers locally in Lugano and Chiasso than you can count. The area is second only to Zurich in the proliferation of financial services. All Tokyo, London and Wall Street publications are available at many stands on the day of publication. Locally you can eat in several hundred ethnic gourmet restaurants and see first run English language films in a movie palace the likes of which no longer exist in most big cities. Most of the action is in Lugano, ten minutes across the lake by 'vaporetto' bus-boat, or over the one mile long causeway by car.

Shopping, dining, night clubbing, golf, horses, tennis clubs, spectator sports, every pleasure known to man is available. Modern hospitals and internationally known clinics attract the wealthiest people of the world to the area for a variety of cures and treatments. As to morality and personal eccentricity, local Italian Swiss are easy-going and more tolerant than their German Swiss brothers fifty miles to the north.

For an inexpensive, stress-free, tax-free life, Dr. Hill suggests, "Move to Campione this year. Buy property soon, before it is over-publicised and discovered." *You could probably make twenty times on your money over the next decade in this semi-autonomous town that practically pays you to live there.*Only a short drive from Italy, France, Austria, Liechtenstein and Germany, Campione is still a sleepy peaceful and unspoiled tax haven. But it appears to be heading rapidly towards becoming another Monaco. The ground floor is now. The present population of 3,000 is just 10 per cent of Monaco's. Monte Carlo has 35,000 people on a similar square mile of waterfront. Campione in 1993 is like Monte Carlo in 1949, before it became 'in' and developed into a mini-Manhattan.

This Special Report gives the who, what, where, when and why. Hill feels that Campione is a great place to escape to, while it is still relatively uncongested. In five or ten years as it becomes overcrowded, it will be the place you can escape from. But your little villa would hopefully be a million dollar hotel or apartment site by then. In the meantime, you have a conveniently located European home base, you can pick up an EC passport and you can enjoy life in Campione, one of the most unusual spots on Earth.

The Campione Report is available from Scope International Ltd., 62 Murray Road, Waterlooville, Hampshire PO8 9JL, UK. Price £60 UK Sterling (or equivalent). See last two pages in this report for ordering details.

ISBN 0 906619 22 X

THE MONACO REPORT

HOW TO BECOME A LEGAL RESIDENT OF TAX-FREE MONTE CARLO, MONACO

5th Edition

by Dr. W.G. Hill

There are many places where you could live and be free of income taxes, inheritance and estate taxes and real estate taxes. But most are isolated, too cold, too hot, too Third World, or simply too dull. Monaco is the only tax haven located a short drive from several truly major cities, and at the same time in a resort area well known for its glitter and the non-stop action of major gambling casinos. It boasts fine beaches, golf and tennis clubs. This report looks at tax havens in general and compares Monaco with the runners-up: Andorra, Bermuda, Campione and Liechtenstein. It provides a simple test to see if Monaco is 'your cup of tea'. Tax havens are discussed in a way that shows how they may be used to advantage by middle class people (not just the very wealthy) fed up with high taxes and government controls. But more importantly, a new possibility is discussed: the option of being a 'Permanent Traveller', spending up to six months a year in the most enjoyable places of the world, being able to avoid taxes entirely because you are legally classified as a tourist. The report also goes into the question of how to earn a living, manage a business, handle investments, form corporations or trusts, etc.

The Monaco Report documents how, contrary to popular belief, it is possible to live in a hotel, eat regularly, and have a pleasant month in Monaco on a budget of £20 a day. But as a practical matter, a liveable apartment with a sea-view will cost about £500 a month – considerably less than half the price of similar accommodation in New York or London. And the weather is far better! There are a few problems in paradise, one of them being the French Government. But for those who read this Special Report, the effect of French fiscal measures can be completely and legally avoided by not making the mistake of transferring substantial assets to Monaco banks and fiduciaries. The moves to win the game are all in *The Monaco Report*.

The surprisingly simple legal steps to take to become a resident and obtain the coveted Monaco Identity Card are revealed. It is absolutely free, the main requirement being the ability to support yourself without taking away a Monegasque's job. There is no net worth requirement and once in Monaco, many interesting jobs and opportunities are available. Also covered are such questions as whether to buy or rent; how to buy a luxury car for less than half the usual price, and register it tax-free in Monaco; exchange controls; meeting new friends or single men and women; why Americans have a particularly good deal in Monaco; even advice on getting a good parking spot . . .

The Monaco Report is masterfully written and is designed to spare many months of seeking answers and save many thousands of dollars getting the wrong ones!

A comprehensive appendix includes: Attorneys, stockbrokers, management, business and finance consultants, banks, medical practitioners, dentists, motor dealers and garages, supermarkets, hotels (with price ranges), restaurants, cinemas and theatres.

ISBN 0 906619 20 3.

The Monaco Report is available from Scope International Ltd., 62 Murray Road, Waterlooville, Hampshire PO8 9JL, UK. Price – £60 UK Sterling (or equivalent) by credit card, cash, cheque or banker's draft. Price includes postage and packing, and please allow 6-8 weeks for surface delivery outside UK. For quicker air mail service add £15 or equivalent (allow 3-4 weeks for delivery). Ordering details and order form are supplied on the last two pages of this Report.

REMEMBER: Consultations with specialists are available to all purchasers and our no nonsense money back guarantee applies to all our publications.

THE LLOYD'S REPORT
HOW TO EARN A SUBSTANTIAL SECOND INCOME UNDERWRITING INSURANCE
6th Edition
by Dr. W.G. Hill

How would you like to earn an additional £10,000+ a year? No investment, time nor expertise is required, but a minimum net worth (or means) of UK £250,000 is needed to qualify. There is no work to do; no expertise is required. Quite simply, you fill out a form, and in due course you become a member or 'Name' at Lloyd's. You could expect an income of up to UK £200,000 per year for the rest of your life; doors will open to excellent asset management opportunities, plus much invaluable business information and social contacts.

But what about the risk? You have read stories about members who have been driven into bankruptcy by their unlimited liability. Let's put those horror stories into perspective: In round numbers, Lloyd's has about 20,000 members. In an average year, a few hundred of them walk away with up to a million dollars in profit (without any investment whatsoever). Thousands of others might deposit cheques in excess of $100,000; and the average Joe Member could expect to make around £30,000 annually from an exposure of £350,000 for which a letter of credit of £136,500 is required. In a bad year like those we have just experienced, 1989 to 1991 (Lloyd's always take 2-3 years to close an account), most Names will have containable losses, others have taken out stop-loss policies to limit their loss to 10 per cent of their total allocation; but some will find themselves writing cheques in excess of $100,000 after experiencing losses on some syndicates in excess of 100 per cent of their individual allocations. In 1993 a £3bn loss was declared for the total market – but still over 30 per cent of names (members) made a profit.

Compare this with an average year in the stock or commodities markets: A very small percentage of the players (usually insiders) make millions or even billions. The majority are lucky to earn 10-20 per cent on capital they are risking. In a bad year like 1987, almost everyone lost from 30 per cent to 100 per cent of their money. In any year, like all gamblers, those on the margin are typically wiped out eventually, with the figure in commodities being around 87 per cent of all leveraged speculators losing 100 per cent (or more) of their capital in four years or less. A typical stock market player lasts only a little longer.

There are no sure things in life, but Lloyd's membership as we explain in more detail in the Report, comes close. No investment, a double return on capital. Every twenty years or so, it is likely that a Name will have to dig in his pocket to cover losses; but this can be hedged by setting up reserves which receive favourable tax treatment in the UK; taking out personal stop-loss insurance; joining mutual insurance pools; or choosing syndicates very carefully with help from experts as well as reputable members agent. Clients of Dr. Hill will probably have to "dig" less deep than the average Name to cover losses because we can recommend experts that can steer Names away from poorly rated syndicates and badly run underwriting agencies.

The bad publicity is really quite unreflective of the true situation. It simply isn't nearly as bad as it is painted. Yet the current rash of newspaper horror stories do provide an opportunity! Faint-hearted, newer, easily panicked members are in fact dropping out like scared, exhausted rabbits. With just a bit more stamina they could finish in the money. Their departures are your opportunity. For the first time in many years, there are many openings on better syndicates. Instead of waiting five or ten years to get a good spread of profitable, highly rated syndicates, a new member today, with proper guidance can position himself on the ground floor. New members can get set for a real whiz-bang ascent when the self-adjusting insurance market recovers and again becomes profitable – as it always does.

Dr. Hill thinks Lloyd's at the bottom, in the midst of all the bad news is a better bet now than at any time since the last trough, in the mid 1960s.

When Hill was first asked by a potential Lloyd's candidate to investigate Lloyd's, he was very skeptical of such a 'perfect arrangement'. However he accepted the challence of doing an in-depth study of Lloyd's as a business opportunity. The client paid $6000 for a Special Report, that, with his permission we have published, now in its sixth edition.

Surprisingly, Hill concluded that although a Lloyd's membership was not a one-way street to riches, it was one of the better and least risky business opportunities in the world today. He discovered a secret about all the bad publicity: It was very much like the frequent public relations releases of a Las Vegas Casino announcing big winners. Insurance underwriting is much like owning a gambling casino. Big losses are good business. Rates are set to cover losses and yield a profit. Without losses there would be no insurance industry. Hill's client eventually joined Lloyd's. This client's later experiences show all the positive and negative aspects of Lloyd's membership.

There were some surprises, and the procedure for becoming a member was an unusual experience, to put it mildly. In many conversations with people connected with Lloyd's the client was discouraged from joining. The reason for this is another secret Hill discovered in the course of his investigation . . . .

Exact steps to be taken and sources to contact are provided in the report including the names, addresses and telephone numbers of all the Underwriting Agencies at Lloyd's. Here is all you need to know. We found this to be possibly the most fascinating of Dr. Hill's superior reports.

ISBN 0 906619 18 1.

The Lloyd's Report is available from Scope International Ltd., 62 Murray Road, Waterlooville, Hampshire PO8 9JL, UK. Price – £60 UK Sterling (or equivalent) by credit card, cash, cheque or banker's draft. Ordering details and order form are supplied on the last two pages of this Report.

REMEMBER: Consultations with specialists are available to all purchasers,we even have a Lloyd's expert, and our no nonsense money back guarantee applies to all our publications.

THE FREE CAR REPORT
HOW TO OWN A NEW LUXURY CAR EVERY YEAR OF YOUR LIFE, TAX FREE
3rd Edition
by Dr. W.G. Hill

In this unique and original report the author shows readers how, during the past thirty years he has owned a Rolls, Ferrari, and several Mercedes – a new one each year – losing absolutely nothing on these fine motor vehicles. Hill shares his secrets explaining how he learned where cars could be bought "tax free" at the lowest factory list prices in the world. He reveals WHY prices in DENMARK are as low as half of what they are in other countries. Yes, the biggest part of this confidential registered report is buying tax-free at Denmark's low prices. Now that you know this secret, why buy our newest special report? The answer is simply that there is more to it than just buying a car in Denmark:

For instance, without knowing what's in our exciting new book, you'd automatically get Danish Tourist license plates expiring in six months. In the process of "exporting" from Denmark, you would lose your price advantage by paying duties easily and legally avoided. After you read this exclusive report you'll know how to get 2 year Danish or cheap renewal tax-free plates in Germany, Andorra, Gibraltar, USA and England. You will be able to use your car legally all over the world!

Another secret is that *you don't have to go to Denmark to get your tax free ultra-cheap car. Your Danish-origin car can be delivered to you* – while you take your summer vacation in say, sunny Spain. This report includes a list of recommended dealers plus warnings about a few sharks. The alternatives – making your next car deal in the Netherlands, Belgium, Switzerland, Gibraltar or Andorra (better for a few brands of cars) are also discussed.

Insurance on your car can cost as much as £4000 per annum, depending upon your driving record and whether you can say the "magic words". *What Magic Words get you 50 per cent OFF ON YOUR INSURANCE,* and a two year license plate instead of six months? You will learn these secrets only in this special report. For instance, W.G. Hill recently paid only £70 per annum for his full-coverage car insurance and £45 for his annual license plates. Do you spend this sort of nominal fund as the entire cost (besides gas and oil) of a brand new car? Finally this special report shows (after a year of fun driving and pride of ownership) *how to sell your car at a considerable profit* over the purchase price. Then you simply repeat the process again and again to have a free luxury car every year of your life!

LIMITATIONS

Can this technique work for everyone? The answer is that it will work for "almost everyone". It will NOT WORK 100 per cent for a 9 to 5 working guy who lives in the country of his origin, has only one passport, and never parks himself or his buggy anywhere outside the town he was born in. As with most Hill techniques, the "free car" gambit works best for PTs who have at least one of the five PT flags, i.e. a secondary residence. Do you spend play-time in a country different from your domicile? Then you can benefit! The scheme will also be more difficult for those who insist upon British style right-hand drive steering wheels. As Hill's technique involves buying in one country tax-free with a low factory list, and selling in another, the choice of cars and sales price-flexibility is restricted with a right-hand drive auto. But for the individual who lives part time outside of the UK and doesn't mind a left hand drive, this scheme will work! More importantly, even for nine-to-fivers who never travel, the techniques explained in this book may be used to make *considerable savings,* even if not realizing the full benefits promised by the title. Any reader should save at least ten times the price of the book, on the purchase, insurance and licensing of every car he buys for the rest of his life. The author feels that this fact makes his new report quite a bargain! We think that as with all of Dr. Hill's original ideas for PTs you'll get more than your money's worth from this special report. If you don't agree, send it back. We promise you a full refund (with a smile)!

ISBN 0 906619 29 7

The Free Car Report is available from Scope International Ltd., 62 Murray Road, Waterlooville, Hampshire PO8 9JL, UK. Price £60 UK Sterling (or equivalent) by credit card, cash, cheque or banker's draft. Price includes postage and packing, and please allow 6-8 weeks for surface delivery outside UK. For quicker air mail service add £15 or equivalent (allow 3-4 weeks for delivery). Ordering details and order form are supplied on the last two pages of this Report.

REMEMBER: Our no nonsense money back guarantee applies to all our publications.

THE CHANNEL ISLAND REPORT
HOW TO ESTABLISH AND MAINTAIN A TAX HAVEN DOMICILE ON A CHANNEL ISLAND (UK) FOR £50 PER MONTH
1st Edition
by Scope International

A businessman, weary of government red tape, lawsuits and domestic problems, arranged to sell his business and investments for a sizeable sum. If he could keep the proceeds he would enjoy financial security with a very comfortable income. But if he had to pay all the required taxes his economic base would be cut in half.

Being both ethical and cautious, he rejected the appeals of tax shelter promoters and schemes that sounded fraudulent. "If only there was a way to keep my hard-earned money working for me instead of seeing it taken away." So he endeavoured to determine whether establishing a tax haven domicile was a good idea for him, and how much time one actually had to spend at such a residence. His findings were:

1. IS MOVING TO A TAX HAVEN LEGAL?
   Generally, yes. Almost all countries permit the free movement of their citizens. In peacetime, most nations also permit assets to be transferred abroad. But more importantly we discovered this basic principle of international law: *A government has jurisdiction (power to control) only over those people and property within its frontiers.* Once someone removes himself and the family jewels from a particular country, for all practical purposes that jurisdiction ends. (Exceptions are deportation and extradition for serious crimes).

2. DOES IT MAKE ECONOMIC SENSE?
   For this particular client, yes indeed! We concluded that anyone who enjoyed travelling a few months a year and who was not absolutely tied down to a nine-to-five job in a high tax country should at least consider tax havens. A mere change of legal address could typically double the income of retirees. In most cases the tax savings alone could finance all travel and living expenses. Greater financial freedom and flexibility are also factors to consider.

3. HOW MUCH TIME MUST ONE SPEND AT A TAX HAVEN?
   You don't have to live there. Domicile is normally a question of personal intention, not physical presence. Thus, a person who calls a certain place 'home' can travel elsewhere for years, but his domicile will stay the same. True, some tax havens, notably Monaco, have fairly strict rules to the effect that to retain a resident's card one must actually be physically present six months a year. But many other tax havens don't issue residence cards or even keep track of their citizens. A domicile with this sort of informal approach is to be preferred. Residence is proved by such things as a mailing address, telephone listing, apartment lease, or house deed, etc.

This particular tax haven is 100 per cent English-speaking, and has far tougher bank-secrecy laws than Switzerland.

The government is perhaps the least intrusive of any nation on earth, and is a protectorate of a major power. It is politically stable, located within commuting distance of Paris and London. It is totally free of crimes of violence or fraud. Communications are excellent. This report contains all the information you will need to know about establishing your own tax haven domicile in this unique location.

ISBN 0 906619 38 6.

The Channel Island Report is available from Scope International Ltd., 62 Murray Road, Waterlooville, Hampshire PO8 9JL, UK. Price – £60 UK Sterling (or equivalent) by credit card, cash, cheque or banker's draft. Price includes postage and packing, and please allow 6-8 weeks for surface delivery outside UK. For quicker air mail service add £15 or equivalent (allow 3-4 weeks for delivery). Ordering details and order form are supplied on the last two pages of this Report.

REMEMBER: Consultations with specialists are available to all purchasers and our no nonsense money back guarantee applies to all our publications.

THE SWISS REPORT
by Marshall J. Langer
2nd Edition for 1993/94

Some countries pride themselves on being 'like Switzerland', but there is only one Switzerland, the most respected small country in the world. *The Swiss Report* gives you an inside look at the country and the institutions that make it tick.

Switzerland is not exactly a tax haven but it is the world's greatest *money haven.* Chances are you already keep some of your money in Swiss banks. *The Swiss Report* takes you inside this country that is deservedly called "the world's safest place for your money."

The report describes Switzerland's banks, its world-renowned bank secrecy, and attempts by other countries to end that secrecy. It discusses the controls that limit non-residents to buying small amounts of Swiss real estate. It describes the companies typically used by investors and how you can save money by using a limited liability company instead of a corporation.

Langer considers Switzerland to be both a tax planner's dream and his nightmare. Correctly used in the way spelled out in the report it can be a base for you to earn money at a tax rate of 11 per cent or less, but it is hard to get that money out of Switzerland without paying a 35 per cent federal tax.

The report tells you how to visit Switzerland, places to visit, where to stay, how to travel around, where to eat. Would you like to stay longer? The report also tells you how to live and work in Switzerland, or retire there. Sure there are restrictions on obtaining permits to live in Switzerland. If it didn't have them, millions more would try to live and work there. Residence permits are difficult to obtain, but not impossible, and *The Swiss Report* tells you how to get them. It even discusses how you can spend up to six months each year in Switzerland as a 'Permanent Traveler' (PT), legally remaining a tourist instead of a taxpayer.

Dr. W.G. (Bill) Hill regards Marshall Langer as his 'tax guru'. Langer is a tax lawyer and the author of several books including the standard reference work on tax havens, *Practical International Tax Planning,* published by New York's Practising Law Institute. After more than thirty years of law practice in Florida, Langer moved to Europe. He lived in Neuchatel, Switzerland for five years and still operates a company from there. Dr. Hill has encouraged Langer to share his know-how about Switzerland with readers of these reports. Langer's clients have willingly paid him large fees for many of the insights he has learned as a Swiss-based international tax planner and which he now shares with you in *The Swiss Report.*

The Report answers these questons:

Is Switzerland freer than the USA or Great Britain?
Should you apply for a resident's permit or live there unofficially, as a PT?
Should you move there at all?
What's the real cost of living?
Regional variations?
How do you avoid or reduce Swiss taxes?
How can you use Swiss bank accounts and the Swiss secrecy laws to your advantage?
How safe and secret really are your financial affairs?
What are the Swiss really like?
Will you have to do military service?
How long before you can apply to be a citizen?
Where can you get a good meal?
Swiss punctuality and other peculiarities – how do they affect you?
Should you buy a home or rent?
How can you benefit from Swiss tax treaties?
Can you survive with just English?
Will Switzerland join the European common market?
Can a foreigner own a Swiss company?
How can you negotiate a flat income tax in advance?

These and many other questions are answered in *The Swiss Report.* We highly recommend it.

ISBN 0 906619 28 9

The Swiss Report is available from Scope International Ltd., 62 Murray Road, Waterlooville, Hampshire PO8 9JL, UK. Price £60 UK Sterling (or equivalent) by credit card, cash, check or banker's draft. Price includes postage and packing, and please allow 6-8 weeks for surface delivery outside UK. For quicker air mail service add £15 or equivalent (allow 3-4 weeks for delivery). Ordering details and order form are supplied on the last two pages of this Report.

REMEMBER: Our no nonsense money back guarantee applies to all our publications.

THE TAX EXILE REPORT
CITIZENSHIP, SECOND PASSPORTS AND ESCAPING CONFISCATORY TAXES
2nd Edition for 1994
Marshall J. Langer

Are you fed up with paying confiscatory taxes? Are you willing to move and to do whatever else may be legally necessary to escape your present tax burden? If so, *The Tax Exile Report* is for you. This report is intended for the small minority of well-to-do individuals who are no longer willing to tolerate increasingly unfair tax systems and are prepared to **vote with their feet.**

Marshall Langer's newly revised report tells you how to overcome the **tax octopus** – eight different criteria used by the United States and other high-tax countries to tax you on your income and your capital. To avoid confiscatory taxes you must eliminate each of the eight tax tentacles, one by one. Langer's report tells you how to do it.

Langer tells you how to change your **residence** and your **domicile,** and when and how to acquire another **nationality**. He explains how to cope with **community property rules**. His report also tells you how to change the **source of your income** and the **location of your assets**. He helps you to **watch your timing** and to deal with problems caused by **family members who remain behind**.

Should you become a **perpetual tourist (PT)** or should you move to a new homeland? The report will help you to make the right choice.

The Tax Exile Report deals with the special problems involved in leaving high-tax countries, including America (the US), Britain, Canada, Germany and the Nordic countries. Langer concentrates on demystifying the US rules and telling you how they really work. He tells you how to plan around the US **anti-expatriation rules** and the departure taxes imposed in other countries. His report devotes twenty chapters to a review of suitable destination countries, describing the benefits and pitfalls of each of them. Surprisingly these include some of the high-tax countries that others are seeking to escape. Langer explains that most high-tax countries play both ends against the middle. They constantly squeeze their captive 'customers' while seeking to attract new investment from abroad.

The depth of coverage can best be seen by reviewing the partial summary of the **table of contents** which follows.

SUITABLE PLACES FOR RESIDENCE, DOMICILE, CITIZENSHIP AND PASSPORTS
MOVING TO AMERICA (the US): Part-Time Residence Is Best, Longer Stays Are Dangerous, New Investor's Immigration Program
MOVING TO AUSTRALIA: Requirements for Business Migration, It is Difficult to Abandon Residence
MOVING TO THE BAHAMAS: Investment Promotion Program, Other Advantages Include No Taxes
MOVING TO BERMUDA: Requirements, Other Advantages Include No Taxes
MOVING TO BRITAIN (the UK): Advantages, Possible Disadvantages, Residency Rules Retained, Domicile Rules May Improve
MOVING TO CANADA: Requirements for Economic Migration, Comparing the US and Canada
MOVING TO CAYMAN: Immigration Quotas, Other Advantages Include No Taxes
MOVING TO THE CHANNEL ISLANDS (Jersey/Guernsey/Sark): Jersey Wants Only the Very Rich, Other Advantages, Possible Residence or Domicile in Sark
MOVING TO COSTA RICA: Requirements for *Pensionado* Status, No Tax on Foreign Income
MOVING TO IRELAND: Advantages
MOVING TO ISRAEL: Shipping Magnate Moves Back to Israel
MOVING TO MALTA: Other Requirements for New Residents, Other Advantages
MOVING TO MONACO: Acquiring Residence Takes Time and Money, Other Requirements, Not for French Citizens, Other Advantages
MOVING TO THE NETHERLANDS ANTILLES (the NA): Advantages for Dutch Emigrants
MOVING TO SWITZERLAND: Retire With a Lump-Sum Tax Deal, Visit as a *PT* for Almost Half of Each Year, You Can Get a Work Permit, Other Advantages
MOVING TO TURKS AND CAICOS: Residence Permits Are Available, Permanent Residence Certificate, Nationality and Belonger Status, Other Advantages Include No Taxes
MOVING TO URUGUAY: Self-Help Program, Investor Program, Other Advantages Include No Income Tax
MOVING TO OTHER EC COUNTRIES (France/Greece/Italy/Portugal/Spain): Millions of *PTs* Live Near the Mediterranean, Homes Are Owned by Offshore Companies, *PTs* Avoid Official Residence, Former Domicile Remains Unchanged
MOVING ELSEWHERE: Tiny Andorra in the Pyrenees, Anguilla – Escaping From Civilization, Antigua Has Beautiful Beaches, Barbados – a Sophisticated Caribbean Island, British Virgin Islands Offers Superb Sailing, Campione Is a Back Door to Switzerland, Isle of Man – Close to the UK, Mauritius – In the Indian Ocean, Mexico Attracts Retired Americans, Montserrat – a Pleasant Caribbean Island, Northern Marianas – a Plan to Save Taxes, Panama as a Place to Retire, Singapore Attracts Hong Kong Chinese, South Africa Has Political Problems, Sri Lanka Is Disturbed Politically, Other Possible Safe Havens
SHOULD *YOU* BECOME A TAX EXILE?
YOUR ULTIMATE ESTATE PLAN
RESOURCE LIST

Why is Marshall Langer uniquely qualified to write this Report?

He is a member of the Florida Bar, and practised law in Miami for more than 35 years. He has worked as an international tax adviser in Europe since 1985, living in Switzerland and in England. He was a partner in the law firm of Shutts & Bowen, Miami, and remains of counsel to that firm. He was also an Adjunct Professor of Law and the University of Miami for many years. In 1990, Langer received the Florida Bar Tax Section's award as **Outstanding Tax Attorney of the Year.**

Dr. Langer is a graduate of the Wharton School of Finance and Commerce of the University of Pennsylvania (B.S. in Economics) and the University of Miami School of Law (J.D. *summa cum laude*). He has lectured extensively at tax institutes and seminars throughout the US and Europe, as well as in Japan, Hong King, Australia, Canada, and the Caribbean. He has written numerous articles on international taxation and books on tax and other subjects. He is the author of *The Swiss Report,* published in 1991 by Scope Books. He is also the author of a leading book on tax havens and how to use them, entitled: *Practical International Tax Planning* (the third edition was published in 1985 and is updated annually). In addition, Langer is co-author (with Rufus Rhoades of Los Angeles) of a five-volume set of books on taxes and tax treaties called: *Rhoades & Langer, Income Taxation of Foreign Related Transactions* (updated four times a year).

The Tax Exile Report by Marshall J. Langer is available from Scope International Ltd. Price £60 ($100). See last two pages in this report for ordering details.

Personal consultations with Dr. Langer are available to all purchasers of *The Tax Exile Report.*

ISBN 906619 34 3

THE TAX HAVEN REPORT
2nd Edition
Adam Starchild

The words "tax haven" bring to mind far off corners of the planet with millionaire populations. This population, of course, spends most of its day drinking daiquiris on the beach, its funds secure in various numbered Swiss bank accounts. Not so, according to Adam Starchild (well, he doesn't refute the daiquiri bit). Tax havens need not be the exclusive refuge of the ultra-rich. People of average means need no longer be captive slaves to the State in today's modern jet-set era. In his newly revised *The Tax Haven Report,* Adam Starchild reveals these secrets of the ultra-rich so that us lesser mortals can take advantage of the many benefits tax havens have to offer.

As modern governments continue to expand and swallow human rights, deficits and taxes grow. All free-minded individuals must seek a means to protect their assets from this monster out of control. As Starchild explains, it is legally possible to pay absolutely no taxes. Your government may want you to think otherwise. The media may love to tattle about the misery of a particular celebrity "tax evader", but a very important point remains unnoticed. While "tax evasion" is illegal, "tax avoidance" is not. This distinction is crucial, and thus Starchild explains it at great length.

Starchild goes on to cover this exhausting subject from start to finish in a clear, easy to understand style. No legal jargon here. He brings over twenty years of experience to the production of this report and doesn't hop on the bandwagons for the latest "fad" tax havens. (It is not commonly known, but tax havens are just as interested in finding you as you are in finding them.) He explains everything from the basic criteria you should use when assessing a tax haven to how you can put them to work to save you that big chunk of your income whisked off each year by Big Brother.

For entrepreneurs and businessmen, he explains the ins and outs of tax haven corporations and trusts, including how they are formed, how they are controlled, where they can be located, and, most importantly, how they can seriously reduce, if not eliminate, the tax burden of your business.

Starchild explains the basics of some of the known and not-so-known tax havens of the world. He divides them into easily identifiable categories, including:

No-tax havens: The Bahamas, Bermuda, The Cayman Islands

Foreign-source-income havens: Panama, Cyprus, Malta, The Isle of Man, Jersey, Guernsey, Gibraltar, Hong Kong

Double-taxation agreement havens: The Netherlands, Austria, Luxembourg

This report also includes detailed chapters on both Liechtenstein and Switzerland. In stark contrast with most tax experts, Starchild successfully argues that Switzerland no longer has a great deal to offer as a tax haven.

This report is essential reading for anyone interested in reducing his tax burden. With over 170 pages of vital information, we are certain that you can develop a successful plan to reduce your tax burden as a result of reading this report. We are so certain that we do not even hesitate to offer it with our standard money-back guarantee. Unless you are absolutely satisfied return it within 28 days for a full refund.

About the Author: Adam Starchild has been a business consultant for nearly two decades. He is the author of over a dozen books, four of which are on tax havens, the earliest having been published in 1978. He has also written hundreds of magazine articles, for journals around the world. Amongst the many publishing his articles have been: The Christian Science Monitor, Credit & Financial Management, International Business, The New York Times, The San Francisco Examiner, Tax Angles, Tax Haven & Shelter Report, Tax Haven News *and* Tax Planning International.

His consulting clients have ranged from wealthy individuals to banks, trust companies, investment companies, book publishers, import-export companies and tour operators. Often critical of the hype and inflated prices from some of the more famous tax havens, Starchild gives you the benefit of his many years hands-on experience in setting up trusts in many countries around the world.

ISBN 0 906619 39 4

The Tax Haven Report is available from Scope International Ltd., 62 Murray Road, Waterlooville, Hampshire PO8 9JL, UK. Price £60 UK Sterling (or equivalent) by credit card, cash, cheque or banker's draft. Price includes postage and packing, and please allow 6-8 weeks for surface delivery outside UK. For quicker air mail service add £15 or equivalent (allow 3-4 weeks for delivery). Ordering details and order form are supplied on the last two pages of this Report.

REMEMBER: Consultations with specialists, including Adam Starchild, are available to all purchasers and our no nonsense money back guarantee applies to all our publications.

HOW TO ORDER:

Each individual leather bound report is £60 or equivalent in any currency. Price includes p&p surface delivery. All orders are despatched immediately, but please allow 6-8 weeks for surface delivery (UK 28 days). For quicker service add £15 for air mail. Bank drafts, travellers' cheques made payable to SCOPE INTERNATIONAL LTD. or currency may be sent. **Or** quote credit card number and expiry date. Telephone and fax orders will be accepted on the numbers given below. If you are not satisfied, your money will be refunded to you in full if you return the undamaged report(s) to us within 28 days of receipt. **Please use the order form on the reverse side of this page.**

Post, Fax or Telephone your order to:-

SCOPE INTERNATIONAL LTD, 62 Murray Road, Waterlooville, Hants. PO8 9JL, Great Britain.
Telephone: (0705) 592255
Fax: (0705) 591975
Outside UK - Dial: International Code + 44-705-592255 (or 591975 for Fax)

SPECIAL OFFER

Save £60!

SPECIAL OFFER TO READERS OF THIS REPORT!

Order any 3 or more of our Special Reports and you may deduct £60 off the total cost, order 6 and you may deduct £135, order 9 and you may deduct £225. Simply tick the Special Offer box on the order form on the reverse side of this page, mark your choice of Reports and deduct £60, £135 or £225 from the total cost of your order.

None of Scope International's Special Reports are subsidised, authorised or encouraged by the organisations, countries or institutions written about. All the author has to sell is good, objective information. Satisfaction is guaranteed. If these reports do not deliver as advertised, they may be returned (uncopied of course) for a refund.

AVOID DELAY
POST, FAX OR PHONE YOUR ORDER TODAY.

LEARN THE SECRETS OF THE SUPER-RICH

PRIORITY ORDER FORM

Mr/Mrs/Miss/Ms ....
(Block Letters Please)

Address ....

....

....

.... Post/Zip Code ....

Please Tick ☐

SAVE £60!

SPECIAL OFFER TO READERS OF THIS REPORT!

Order any 3 or more of Dr. Hill's Special Reports and you may deduct £60 off the total cost. Simply tick the box on the left, mark your choice of Reports and deduct £60 from the total cost of your order. Order 6 and you may deduct £120. Order 9 and you may deduct £225.

Please Tick			Total
☐	**Think Like A Tycoon**	**£60**	
☐	**The Andorra & Gibraltar Report**	**£60**	
☐	**The Free Car Report**	**£60**	
☐	**PT – Volume I**	**£60**	
☐	**PT – Volume II**	**£60**	
☐	**The Passport Report**	**£60**	
☐	**The Lloyd's Report**	**£60**	
☐	**The Monaco Report**	**£60**	
☐	**The Campione Report**	**£60**	
☐	**The Swiss Report**	**£60**	
☐	**The Tax Exile Report**	**£60**	
☐	**The Channel Island Report**	**£60**	
☐	**The Tax Haven Report**	**£60**	

Please charge my (delete as necessary):
Visa/Access/Mastercard/Eurocard/AMEX/Diners

Signature ....

My card number is: ....

IMPORTANT Please quote expiry date: ....

Order Summary	
TOTAL GOODS	
LESS £60, £135 OR £225 SPECIAL OFFER DISCOUNT	
SUB-TOTAL	
AIRMAIL CHARGE £15 ($25) (SURFACE & UK - NO CHARGE)	
TOTAL	
CHEQUE ENCLOSED PAYABLE TO SCOPE BOOKS LTD	

NO NONSENSE MONEY BACK GUARANTEE

For Office use only	
DR	DD
CHG	MTD